TETRAGRAM
The Most Enduring Name

MW00878363

By Lew White

A Name Hidden For Ages
**"My people shall know My Name in that day,
For I am the One Who Is speaking. See, it is I."**
YashaYahu / Isaiah 52:6
This statement indicates most people will not know the Name,
And their teachers have intentionally hidden it.
His treasured possession meditates on His Name,
and they speak to one another.
Malaki 3:16-18

YOD-HAY-UAU-HAY
Letters read from right-to-left:

Printed and eBook available at Amazon
Search: author Lew White

TETRAGRAMMATON
The Most Enduring Name In The Universe

The Tetragrammaton Written in Bedrock

A life-sized print of the Los Lunas Stone is used as a back-drop in many videos by this author on youtube. The authentic Hebrew script is on this stone.

The Name is the Stone the builders rejected.

CONTENTS

In the first Commandment, the first 3 words are:

ツＺㄣＣＡ　ㄣＹㄣＺ　ＺツツＡ

ANOKI YAHUAH ALAHIK
(I AM YAHUAH YOUR ALAH)

We are going to find out Who that is in this book.

YAHUAH: 4 VOWELS

TRANSLITERATING: THE FOUR VOWELS OF THE NAME
Transliteration uses letters to make a word *sound* the same using foreign scripts.

Natanyahu hears his name perfectly pronounced by those of foreign languages, because names are not *translated*, but *transliterated*.

Vowels are sounded using only the mouth cavity and breath. What is a vowel, and how do they differ from consonants?

A vowel is a letter sounded <u>without</u> the lips, lower lip with upper teeth, closed teeth, hissing, tongue on the roof of the mouth, or guttural stop in the throat. The shape of the mouth cavity is used. If we hear buzzing, hissing, clicking, or the tongue stops the air as in the word *giggle*, you are making the sound of a consonant. A E I O U are vowels, not consonants. The Name of our Creator is written in four vowels: yod-hay-uau-hay, sounded as YAHUAH, not *YEHOVAH*. *"VEE"* is not a letter in the Tetragrammaton, yod-hay-uau-hay. The Latin letter V sounded as our U.

VENUS (a false deity) was pronounced *UENUS*.

TRANSLITERATIONS

	6,823	216	2	1
	YAHUAH	YAHUSHA	YAHUSHUA	Y'SHUA
HEBREW	ⱻYⱻꓭ	OWYⱻꓭ	OYWYⱻꓭ	OYWꓭ
ARAMAIC	הוהי	עשוהי	עושוהי	עושי
GREEK	IAOUE	IHSOUS		
LATIN	IEHOUAH	IESU		

AT HEBREWS 4 AND ACTS 7 THE SAME GREEK LETTERING IS USED
FOR "JOSHUA" AND "JESUS" - IHSOUS
THIS IS CONFIRMATION BOTH WERE CALLED YAHUSHA IN HEBREW
TORAH INSTITUTE

The Greek letters **IAOUE** were used to transliterate

the Name of YAHUAH.

The niqqud marks are an 8th century CE attempt to control the way words are spoken. The Dead Sea Scrolls (DSS) have no such marks on them.

The marks were added by Masoretes, a Karaite sect of traditionalists, who did not want the Name to be spoken aloud. The letters of Eberith / Hebrew give us all we need to utter the words. They feel the Name is so set-apart it should never be mentioned on human lips, when in fact they are showing their disrespect.

"What is highly thought of men is an abomination in the sight of Alahim." Luke 16:14

YAHUAH or AHAYAH?

AHAYAH ASHER AHAYAH (Ex. 3:14-15) means *"I will be who I will be."*

ASHER means *"who."* *"I will be who I will be"* is Yahuah's response to Mushah's question, *"What is His Name, what shall I tell them?"* Ex. 3:13 Mushah's mother's name expressed the Name **Yah** in it.

H3115, **YOKEBED:** *"Yahuah is esteem,"* not Ahayah is esteem. When Anosh called on the Name (Barashith / Genesis 4:26) it reads **Yahuah** in the Eberith text, not **ahayah**. Yahuah said, *"I am Yahuah, that is My Name"* (YashaYahu 42:8) and

"I am Yahuah your Alahim" repeatedly. The Name is used more than any other word; I've counted it to be written 6,823 times in the TaNaK.

*[TaNaK is an acronym standing for **Torah, Nabim,** and **Kethubim.** In translation this acronym stands for Instruction, Prophets, and Writings.]*

We have inherited lies and misunderstandings based on the misplaced ideas of men *long-dead.*

Teachers today defend their errors as they attempt to justify their traditions.

Our teachers are confused, and their confusion spreads like gangrene throughout the body. Yahusha

came in His Father's Name. There is no deliverance in any other Name, nor any other deliverer besides Him. There is no one like Him.
(see YashaYahu 43:11, Acts 4:12).

Proverbs 30:4: *"What is His Name, and what is His Son's Name, if you know it?"*
YashaYahu (Isaiah) 53 was the very first Scripture I read directly for myself, and it woke me up in 1985.
I wondered who *the LORD* was, and looked at the Preface to discover the translators stated they had obliterated the Name, and used a *device* in its place due to the long-standing tradition.
Traditions became their path to follow, not the intentions of Yahuah.
LORD *translated* back to Eberith as a name is beth-ayin-lamed: **BEL**.
The controversy between AliYahu (aka Elijah) and the priests of BEL at Mt. Karmel (1 Kings 18) concerned this same argument. The world has become more confused by those more concerned with teaching their traditions than teaching what Yahuah wants us to obey. These same teachers demand a tithe, but refuse to teach the Commandments.
The Name was replaced in the Greek as **KYRIOS** (lord), and then Latin as **DOMINUS** (lord).
Gutenberg's printing press made mass produced books possible in 1450. The *Age of Colonization* was in full-swing, resulting in the *Anglican Catholic KJV exporting the English word LORD everywhere their colonies existed.*
Foreigners learned to speak English by reading from the 1611 KJV. Today the world is learning the Name through the message of AliYahu.
At 1 Kings 18, AliYahu told the people if BEL is alahim, then serve him; but BEL failed to show up.

Yahuah is about to come with fire to pour out His wrath on *all who do not know Him*, nor He them. Who are the nations of the world likely to **call** on as the plagues, earthquakes, storms, fires, and meteors are unleashed at the end of days? YashaYahu / Is. 28:16-19:

*"Therefore thus said Aduni Yahuah, 'See, I am laying in Tsiun a **Stone** for a foundation, a tried **Stone**, a precious **corner-stone**, a settled foundation. He who trusts shall not hasten away. And I shall make lawfulness the measuring line, and obedience the plummet. And the hail shall sweep away the refuge of lies, and the mayim overflow the hiding place. And your covenant with death shall be annulled, and your vision with the grave not stand. When an overflowing scourge passes through, then you shall be trampled down by it. As often as it passes through it shall take you, for it shall pass through every morning, and by yom and by lailah. And it shall be only trembling to understand the message."*

In the Preface of the NASB, they admit the Name is *most significant*, and it is *inconceivable* for anyone to think of not using the proper designation. Then, they explain they *did* what they said is *inconceivable*:

NASB - PRINCIPLES OF TRANSLATION

The Proper Name of God in the Old Testament: In the Scriptures, the name of God is most significant and understandably so. It is inconceivable to think of spiritual matters without a proper designation for the Supreme Deity. Thus the most common name for deity is God, a translation of the Hebrew *Elohim*. The normal word for Master is Lord, a rendering of *Adonai*. There is yet another name which is particularly assigned to God as His special or proper name, that is, the four letters YHWH (Exodus 3:14 and Isaiah 42:8). This name has not been pronounced by the Jews because of reverence for the great sacredness of the divine name. Therefore, it was consistently pronounced and translated LORD. The only exception to this translation of YHWH is when it occurs in immediate proximity to the word Lord, that is, *Adonai*. In that case it is regularly translated GOD in order to avoid confusion.

The Stone the builders rejected is the Name of Yahuah.
BARUK HABA BASHEM YAHUAH
Psalm 118:26 / Mt. 23:39

The First Followers Of Yahusha Used The Name

Stephen was stoned because he used the Name, and Shaul was sent into assemblies *to arrest Natsarim for calling on the Name.*

2000 years ago, pronouncing the Name was considered blasphemy, and incurred the death penalty for those who dared to speak it.

Tradition dictated that alternate words be used in place of the written Name, such as ADUNI (aka Adonai). The word *Adonai* is still used in most cases even today when teachers quote from Scriptures aloud. It's popular to circumlocute (talk-around) the real Name is to substitute it by saying *HA SHEM*, meaning *the Name.* This is a pretense of pomposity, since anyone using alternate words is openly displaying how they disdain the Name, and intimidate those who use it. Acts 9:13-14 gives us insight into the severe treatment of those that called on the Name in the assemblies. Yahusha spoke to one of His Natsarim about Shaul, a man sent by the Sanhedrin to arrest and execute those who called on the Name.

To get some sense of what the first Natsarim were facing, here is the context of Acts 9 when Shaul met Yahusha on the road to Damascus:

[Note: the word Aduni means *my lord*; it is not used as a name]

"But Shaul, still breathing threats and murder against the talmidim of Aduni, having come to the high priest, asked from him letters to the assemblies of Damascus, so that if he found any who were of the way, whether men or women, to bring them bound to Yerushalim. And it came to be, that as he journeyed, he came near Damascus, and suddenly a light

flashed around him from the heaven. And he fell to the ground, and heard a voice saying to him, 'Shaul, Shaul, why do you persecute Me?' [Spoken in Hebrew; see Acts 26:14] And he said, 'Who are You Aduni?' And Aduni said, 'I am Yahusha, Whom you persecute. It is hard for you to kick against the goads.' Both trembling and being astonished, he said, 'Aduni, what do You wish me to do?' And Aduni said to him, 'Arise and go into the city, and you shall be told what you have to do.' And the men journeying with him stood speechless, hearing indeed the voice but seeing no one. And Shaul arose from the ground, but when his eyes were opened he saw no one. And leading him by the hand they brought him into Damascus. And he was 3 Yomim [days] without sight, and did not eat nor drink. And there was at Damascus a certain Talmid named Kananyah. And Aduni said to him in a vision, 'Kananyah!' And he said, 'Here I am, Aduni.' And Aduni said to him, 'Arise and go to the street called Straight, and seek in the house of Yahudah for one called Shaul of Tarsus, for look, he is praying, and has seen in a vision a man named Kananyah coming in and laying his hand on him, so as to see again.' And Kananyah answered, 'Aduni, I have heard from many about this man, how many evils he did to Your qodesh ones in Yerushalim, and here he has authority from the chief priests to bind all those calling on Your Name.' But Aduni said to him, 'Go, for he is a chosen vessel of Mine to bear My Name before guyim, kings, and the children of Yisharal. For I shall show him how much he has to suffer for My Name.' And Kananyah went away and went into the house. And laying his hands on him he said, 'Brother Shaul, Aduni Yahusha, who appeared to you on the way as you came, has sent

10

me, so that you might see again and be filled with the Ruach ha Qodesh.' And immediately there fell from his eyes, as it were scales, and he received his sight. And rising up, he was immersed."
Acts 9:1-18 BYNV Kindle eBook

Today, the *last Natsarim* are **shouting** the Name from the rooftops. We can't stop talking about the Name; it's like a burning fire in our bones if we try to hold it back, just as YirmeYahu described it at chapter 20:9.

TETRAGRAMMATON MEANING
The word **tetragrammaton** means *four letters*. This Greek word is referring to the four letters **yod-hay-uau-hay** (YHUH). These are four Eberith / Hebrew vowels that produce the transliteration YAHUAH using the Latin alphabet. A name should be written in foreign scripts in such a way that it sounds identical to the original when spoken.

In the eBook version, the links shown are active for you to do further research. Compare the scripts of Eberith, Aramith, Greek, and Latin, and restore purified lips to all people so they may call on the Name of YAHUAH.

The inspired Word of Yahuah tells us He would do this (ZefanYah 3:9), and many would do research in the last days (Danial 12).
fossilizedcustoms.com/transliteration.html

The First Commandment

"I am **Yahuah** your Alahim who brought you out of the land of Mitsrayim, out of the house of bondage. You have no other alahim against My face."
The first three Hebrew words in this opening statement are:

ＹＺ𝟯𝐶𝟒 𝟯Ｙ𝟯Ｚ Ｚ𝐘𝐘𝟒
ANOKI YAHUAH ALAHIK
(I AM YAHUAH YOUR ALAH)

Three words can mean a great deal; like *"I LOVE YOU."* As important as those three words are, there are another three words even greater.

These three words are used over 300 times in Scripture, and the Ten Commandments begin with them. *Why do pastors not teach this?*

They don't know the Name of the Creator, nor teach His Commandments. They are not Yahuah's servants, but serve a being who hides his identity. They want the tithe, but do not teach the Commandments of Yahuah.

Natsarim guard the **Name** and the **Word** as watchmen, and we were given orders to teach all nations to guard these with diligent obedience.

The next page illustrates each word in real Eberith (Hebrew) script.

The text is read from right-to-left, and you will see the real words that Yahuah wrote with His Own finger. There is a letter chart on the back cover of this book for a reference guide to for studying more closely.

If you study, you will be equipped to teach. The world has been deceived by teachers who desire to be teachers of Turah, but do not know they need to get rid of the leaven (traditions) put in their minds by men first. They teach only the rules and traditions of men, not the Words that will never pass away.

Google: BYNU
torahzone.net

I AM YAHUAH ALAHIM-OF YOU WHO BROUGHT YOU OUT FROM LAND OF MITSRAYIM FROM HOUSE OF

SLAVERIES. NOT HE SHALL BE TO YOU ALAHIM OTHER ONES BEFORE FACE OF ME

NOT YOU MAKE FOR SELF IDOL OR ANY IMAGE THAT IN SKIES FROM ABOVE OR THAT

ON ARETS FROM BENEATH OR THAT IN WATERS FROM BENEATH TO ARETS NOT YOU BOW

TO THEM AND NOT YOU WORSHIP THEM FOR I AM YAHUAH AL OF YOU AL JEALOUS, PUNISHING

SIN OF FATHERS ON CHILDREN TO THIRDS AND TO FOURTH TO ONES HATING ME BUT SHOWING LOVE

O THOUSANDS TO ONES LOVING ME AND TO ONES GUARDING OF COMMANDS OF ME. NOT YOU TAKE NAME YAHUAH

ALAHIM OF YOU FOR RUIN FOR NOT HE HOLD GUILTLESS YAHUAH WHO TAKES NAME OF HIM

FOR RUIN. TO REMEMBER DAY OF THE SHABATH TO SEPARATE: SIX OF DAYS YOU SHALL LABOR

AND YOU SHALL DO ALL OF WORK OF YOU BUT DAY OF THE SEVENTH IS SHABATH TO YAHUAH ALAHIM OF YOU

NOT YOU DO ANY OF WORK YOU OR SON OF YOU OR DAUGHTER OF YOU MANSERVANT OF YOU

OR MAIDSERVANT OF YOU OR ANIMAL OF YOU OR ALIEN OF YOU WHO WITHIN GATES OF YOU

FOR SIX OF DAYS HE MADE YAHUAH THE SKIES AND THE ARETS x 4

THE SEA AND ALL THAT IN THEM BUT HE RESTED ON THE DAY THE SEVENTH

FOR THIS HE BARUK YAHUAH DAY OF THE SHABATH AND HE MADE SEPARATE HIM

HONOR FATHER OF YOU AND MOTHER OF YOU THAT THEY MAY BE LONG DAYS OF YOU

IN THE LAND THAT YAHUAH ALAHIM OF YOU GIVING TO YOU

NOT YOU MURDER NOT YOU BREAK WEDLOCK NOT YOU STEAL

NOT YOU GIVE AGAINST NEIGHBOR OF YOU TESTIMONY DECEPTIVE

NOT YOU COVET HOUSE OF NEIGHBOR OF YOU NOT YOU COVET WIFE OF NEIGHBOR OF YOU

OR MANSERVANT OR MAIDSERVANT OR OX OR DONKEY OR ANYTHING OF YOUR NEIGHBOR

This is the Way, walk in it.

The Tetragrammaton - Four Vowels

Vowels are sounded using only the mouth cavity and breath.

What is a vowel, and how are vowels different from consonants?

The vowel is a letter sounded without the use of the lips, lower lip with upper teeth, closed teeth, hissing, tongue on the roof of the mouth, or guttural stop in the throat. Only the shape of the mouth cavity is used. If we hear buzzing, hissing, clicking, or the tongue stops the air (as in the word "giggle," you are making the sound of a consonant.

Consonants are very different from vowels.

The Name of our Creator is written in four vowels: yod-hay-uau-hay, sounded as YAHUAH, not YEHOVAH. Watch video: *(links active in eBook)*
https://youtu.be/wRsfDS0yw6g

"VEE" is not the letter in the Tetragrammaton, the Latin letter V is sounded as a U. The Greek letters IAOUE transliterate YAHUAH quite well, but YEHOVAH as read today has several influences from the past.

Masoretes, a Karaite sect established in the 8th century, introduced their imaginary niqqud marks to steer the phonology of the Hebrew (EBERITH) language. Masorah means *tradition*. The Masoretes based their name on this word. Tradition prohibited the uttering the Name aloud, and anyone doing so was considered to be a blasphemer. The Masoretes' new marks helped to control the way words are spoken when read aloud. The world inherited their influences, so we see their effects in concordances, dictionaries, and encyclopedias all around the world today.

The Dead Sea Scrolls have no such marks.

The niqqud marks were invented in Babylon, a city literally meaning *confusion*, under a Caliph. The vowels of the Eberith language are written letters, which show us how to utter the words.

My Messenger
The message of AliYahu, to the priests of Bel (Baal) and Asherah, sounded nonsensical to them.
Read about this encounter at Mt. Karmel. (1Kings 18)
AliYahu (aka Elijah) means *"Yahuah is my Alahim."*
At Malaki (my messenger) 4:1-6 contains a message to all the inhabitants of the Earth, and is given for the last days prior to the Day of Yahuah.
AliYahu's message is now being *transmitted* around the world, and when understood by the hearer, it will tingle their ears. A global crematorium is being prepared for all the disobedient inhabitants of the Earth. YashaYahu / Is. 24 & Mt. 24 concur.

The teachers of tradition are highly agitated.
Their agitation seems to be caused by a fear that people will stop listening to them. The Truth will set us free from the traditions handed-down from centuries of rules imposed by men. The human heart is deceptive.
Our enemy desires to keep it that way. The Word of Yahuah is the Truth.
"And whether you turn to the right or to the left, your ears will hear a Voice behind you saying, 'This is the way, walk in it.'" - YashaYahu 30:21

Is there any higher level of blasphemy imaginable than changing the Name of the Creator, the Sovereign of Esteem into the meaning of a word AliYahu settled at Mt. Karmel? At 1 Kings 18, AliYahu told the people if BEL is alahim, then serve him.

It appears we need another Mt. Karmel to settle the matter. The world does not know Yahuah yet, but all people need to decide WHO is the true Maker of Heaven and Earth. Our fathers have inherited nothing but lies according to YirmeYahu 16:19.

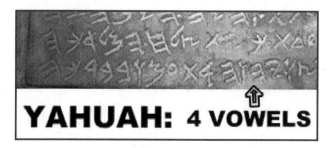

Not Mentioning His Name Is Like A Fire Shut Up In My Bones

YirmeYahu 20:9 says not mentioning the Name became like a fire shut up in his bones. YashaYahu 24 should be the next thing to read because another fire is promised for breaking the eternal Covenant. The Name is a prominent component in the first four of the Ten Commandments. Opening an exhaustive concordance will immediately show us how many times the true Name was removed from all the translations.

The Natsarim Writings are warning letters to guard Yahusha's Commandments, or perish. 1 Yn. 2:4 is very clear, but many passages have been misunderstood by lawless teachers.
The Messiah they are expecting will never come;
The Messiah that is coming they've never expected.
Danial 12:1-4 is what Yahusha was talking about at Mt. 24:20:
"At that time Mikal, the great prince who protects your people, will arise. There will be a time of distress such as has not happened from the

beginning of nations until then. But at that time your people—everyone whose name is found written in the book—will be delivered.

Multitudes who sleep in the dust of the earth will awake: some to everlasting life, others to shame and everlasting contempt. Those who are wise will shine like the brightness of the heavens, and those who lead many to righteousness, like the stars for ever and ever.

But you, Danial, roll up and seal the words of the scroll until the time of the end. Many will search back and forth, and knowledge will increase."

We're getting a second chance to get the right answer. Do we trust that Yahuah's Word is eternal, or do we listen to the world's teachers telling us His Word has changed, is too difficult, and is not eternal?

"Repent, for the Reign of Yahuah draws near."
Mt. 3:2, Mt. 4:17, Mk. 1:15

Listen to the Words of Scripture; the Creator of the universe is telling you something very important. What He is saying is quite different than what you commonly hear from those who claim to teach His Word.

He spoke to our ancestors through the prophets at many times and in various ways, but in these last days He has spoken to us in His Son.

Be careful how you listen.

The translations follow the errors of previous translations. When people around the world became familiar with the errors, the restoration efforts threatened the authority of the teachers, so Truth-bearers are targeted as heretics. Today, anyone can test what they are hearing by searching Interlinear translations on line. With the Mind of Yahusha, we receive discernment, and the Truth will come through for us.

Yahusha wants His Natsarim to warn the pastors and those they are leading astray, but to do so in His love. As disgusting as human traditions are to Yahusha, someone has to be sent to tell them.
If not us, *who?* If not now, *when?*
What men cherish are abominations to Yahuah (see Luke 16:14-15).

REDEMPTION
We are transformed by trusting only in the blood of Yahusha. The renewed Covenant in His blood cancels the penalty of death for our sins. It makes the old covenant obsolete. The old covenant was the animal blood offered by the former priests, and the instructions were hand-written on a scroll and placed beside the ark – see Dt. 31:26. The old covenant is not the Ten Commandments, nor the Scriptures (Genesis to Malaki), although this is what the world has been programmed to believe. We should not listen to men's interpretations, but read the Word for ourselves. The Truth will set us free from men's puffed-up ideas (leaven).
Can we know what a book is about without reading it? People have told me how they know all about the Scriptures of Truth because someone told them all about it. They had never read it for themselves.

A Riddle: *The Mark of the Beast*
The "mark" of the beast is a sign expressed outwardly in those who don't have **wisdom** (Torah), and it's a riddle which cannot be solved without it. The beast is the world order which trains Earth's inhabitants and controls behavior in all cultures since Babel. Its **mark** can only be discerned with wisdom, and is concerned with *"buying and selling."*
Those without the beast's mark are obedient to Torah, and **do not buy** and **sell** because they know not to do so on certain days by *Yahuah's instructions.*
Not having Yahuah's instructions, a person has the mark of the world order, and lacks wisdom. Yahuah's mark contrasts with the beast's mark.
Yahuah sign of the eternal Covenant is Shabath, a day we who know Him do not travel, work, or transact (buy and sell).
fossilizedcustoms.com/mark.html

Obedience Is Easier
In the world-to-come the dogs will not be allowed to enter the Presence of Yahusha and His chosen, obedient ones.
The choice to be a dog or a true obedient one in this world is open to all. The same deception used against us in the Garden of Eden is still working perfectly for the dragon. If we obey the Word of Yahuah, we are thought of as heretics who reject the authority of those teaching us. If we listen to teachers of lawlessness, we are the same as the first woman, who was deceived. Choose eternal life; don't fail a second time to recognize the schemes of the dragon.

Paul's Letters Are Twisted By Lawless Men
Paul's former way of living embraced the leaven of the Pharisees, and he called that way of living "the

traditions of the fathers." The "circus fathers" misinterpreted Paul, just as Peter said the lawless would do. In their misunderstanding of Paul, the way of Truth has been severely maligned, but not through any fault of our beloved brother Paul. Paul taught obedience, and rejected the added teachings of men. This has gone undetected for too long.
fossilizedcustoms.com/shaul.html

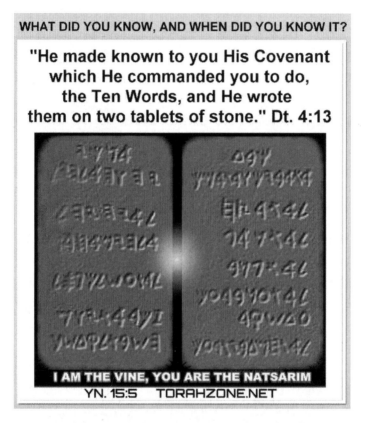

WHAT DID YOU KNOW, AND WHEN DID YOU KNOW IT?

"He made known to you His Covenant which He commanded you to do, the Ten Words, and He wrote them on two tablets of stone." Dt. 4:13

I AM THE VINE, YOU ARE THE NATSARIM
YN. 15:5   TORAHZONE.NET

The Eternal Covenant - What Is It?
The most ridiculous question is the one that is never asked.
Malaki 4:1-6 explains the reason the fire is coming upon the disobedient. One of the first questions my wife and I asked over 35 years ago was "what are we supposed to obey?" We searched for the real Truth. The pastor didn't have a specific answer, so we turned to the Word of Yahuah, and we found it.

We have to be careful how we listen.

The traditions are men's teachings; but the Ten Commandments are forever. Eccl. 12:13-14 says they are for all mankind to obey.

Somehow programming taught a different way, but we heard the Word, and now we love obedience. Why not try it, and see if it is good, or bad? Where can we find them, across the sea? They've been with us all along, but men's teachings have banned them. They say, *"swerve from that path!"*

YashaYahu 51:7 says, **"Listen to Me, you who know obedience, a people in whose heart is My Torah; do not fear the reproach of mere mortals, nor listen to their insults!"**

Based on the Word of Yahuah alone, do Christians have any sort of relationship (covenant, agreement) with Yahuah, *or have they been programmed to think they do?*

The Core War: *What Is It?*

It's a war *against the Eternal Covenant* we were all born into, and we didn't know it. People start out upside-down, and Truth sounds ridiculous to them. This book helps expose this war; some can see the war, and others cannot.

The war is between the Truth and the Traditions taught by men. When someone turns from the idolatry of birthdays, Halloween, Christmas, egg hunts, Valentine's Day, Sunday (none of which are secular, but adopted from paganism), or they stop eating pigs, their behavior draws fiery arrows from those who knew how they used to live.

Are the dietary instructions still binding?

Yes, read YashaYahu (aka Isaiah) 66:17.

The Day of Yahuah will result in the destruction of

most inhabitants of the Earth, having been completely misled by those who have been teaching them lies. This is confirmed by YirmeYahu 16:19 and Malaki 4:1-6. Yahusha warned us of all this at Mt. 5:19. Link to youtube video about the Core War: **https://youtu.be/yVAFP4DjrLI**

Malaki 4:1-6 explains the reason the REAL fire is coming upon the disobedient.

WHY THEY CANNOT UNDERSTAND US
We live because the Life-Giver has breathed His life into us. We have the fragrance of the knowledge of Yahusha, and we want to share it with all we encounter.
We awakened after He prepared our hearts to seek Him through His Word, and it changed our perspective to His. He made us hungry for Truth. Others are not there yet; all they perceive is a zealousness growing in us they cannot possibly comprehend while they remain in the mind of the flesh.
Yahusha draws them to Himself through His ambassadors. His fruits will increasingly show themselves in our behavior. Yahusha will show us how and when to plant His Word in them, and then as a farmer waits for the harvest, He will water and provide nourishment. It's His garden.
When I turned away from the debauchery, my closest relatives thought I was *coo-coo-for-cocoa-puffs*. We have only received what we've been given, and we ate His Word because we were hungry for it. Our close friends and relatives will avoid us if we don't show His joy, so sometimes He makes us be quiet around them. In recent years, after I shared the Name and the importance of obeying the eternal

Covenant with my family, my wife developed 4th-stage cancer due to the stress of Internet slander, and the shunning from all our relatives. During her treatments for cancer, *death came for my parents, my next-younger brother, two aunts, and four uncles.* My wife Phyllis is now completely cured because Yahusha has restored her to serve Him to reach many more who are hungry for Truth. If people aren't hungry, we cannot expect them to desire true food (Truth).

2 Korinthians 2:15-16 helps us understand what is going on:

"Because we are to Yahuah the fragrance of Mashiak among those who are being delivered and among those who are perishing. To the one we are the smell of death to death, and to the other the fragrance of life to life. And who is competent (equipped) **for these?"**

Outside Are The Dogs

At Revelation 22, *"enchanting with drugs"* is often called *"drug sorcery."*

Enchanting with hallucinogenic plants is a pagan practice with the objective being to achieve a higher meditative state. *This subjects a person to become demonically possessed.* We are to stay sober, and be filled with the Mind of Yahusha's Ruach, not drunk or high (Eph. 5:18).

With or without drugs, all forms of divination are sorcery. Necromancy, appealing / praying to the dead for assistance, is *sorcery.* A few examples are: *horoscopes* (hour-watching using astrology), *scrying* (gazing into balls or pools), *prayer beads, seances* (a sitting) to contact spirits, *automatic writing* using **ouija** boards - the French and German for *"yes, yes,"* blowing out candles on cakes and making secret wishes to genies, and *reading palms*.

All of these are an abomination to Yahuah.

Spiritualism of any kind, or serving other deities other than Yahuah, are idolatry.

Yahuah warned us not to learn their ways, nor serve Him in their ways.

fossilizedcustoms.com/christmas.html

What do you think Yahuah will do to those who *do* these things, *or teach them to children?*

The biggest problem all people have to overcome
(including <u>all</u> Christian denominations):

IDOLATRY

It's mankind's most prominent activity, and drives the world economy.

Their teachers have instilled the idea in them that the Ten Commandments are a curse, and the whole world has fallen very far from Yahuah's intended way of living. The Ten Commandments teach us to love Yahuah and our neighbor, and there is no better example than Yahusha, the Word made flesh.

IDOLATRY

MANKIND'S MOST PROMINENT ACTIVITY

MANKIND'S DEFINITION
Extreme admiration, love, or revering of something or someone; worship of a physical object or person;

YAHUAH'S DEFINITION
Setting one's thoughts or actions on anything above Yahuah. He gives an example for us from His prophets, such as YashaYahu (Isaiah) 44:16.

IDOL EXAMPLES: politicians / rulers; movie or music idols; statues, pillars, toasting with drinks; prayers to any entities other than Yahuah, spirits, dead people (necromancy, beads). Expressions we hear used all the time in conversations, and the things we run out to buy and decorate with show how invested we are in all the witchcraft, and hardly ever associate them with idolatry: rosaries, steeples horseshoes and rabbits' feet for good luck - bringing trees into our homes to celebrate a birthday, Black F-day, "let's keep our fingers crossed," horoscopes, palmistry, fortune cookies, baking cakes for

IDOLATRY
MANKIND'S MOST PROMINENT ACTIVITY

birthdays, cone hats, toasting, blowing-out candles, wishes, eggs in baskets and rabbits in the spring, sunrise services, giving candy to costumed children on the day of the dead, Valentine's Day gifts, cards, hearts, and using decorations that remind everyone that we encourage the idolatry that drives the world's economy. The golden cup of Babel has caused madness!

DRIVING THE WORLD ECONOMY

Every merchant prospers from the fertility celebrations that hardly anyone perceives because they are all hypnotized from a lifetime of exposure to the traditions handed-down from our fathers to children. **Idolatry** is exactly what Yahusha referred to as *stumbling blocks* at Mt. 18:3-8. Idolatry is taught to children, and passes into each new generation through family bonding.

Yahuah is sending the plagues now, but most people remain clueless to why. Revelation 9:20 "And the rest of mankind, who were not killed by these plagues, did not repent of the works of their hands, that they should not worship the demons, and idols of gold, and of silver, and of brass, and of stone, and of wood, which are neither able to see, nor to hear, nor to walk. Merchants exploit the wormwood that causes the masses to stay drunk on the idolatrous fertility traditions.

page 1 of a 4-page tract you may download free at
www.torahzone.net

MANKIND'S DEFINITION OF IDOLATRY
Extreme admiration, love, or revering of something or

someone; worship of a physical object or person

YAHUAH'S DEFINITION OF IDOLATRY

Setting one's thoughts or actions on anything above Yahuah. He gives an example for us from His prophets, such as YashaYahu (Isaiah) 44:16.

IDOL EXAMPLES: politicians / rulers; movie or music idols; statues, pillars, toasting with drinks; prayers to any entities other than Yahuah, spirits, dead people (necromancy, beads). Expressions we hear used all the time in conversations, and the things we run out to buy and decorate with show how invested we are in all the witchcraft, and hardly ever associate them with idolatry:

rosaries, holy water, seances, bowing to statues, steeples, horseshoes and rabbits' feet for good luck bringing trees into our homes to decorate, celebrate a birthday, Black F-day, "let's keep our fingers crossed," horoscopes, palmistry, fortune cookies, baking cakes for birthdays, cone hats, toasting, blowing-out candles, wishes, eggs in baskets and rabbits in the spring, sunrise services, giving candy to costumed children on the day of the dead, Valentine's Day gifts, cards, hearts, using decorations that remind everyone that we encourage the idolatry that drives the world's economy, and more – simply keeping silent is a form of endorsement. Lift up your voice like a trumpet, and declare what they are doing is an abomination to Yahuah (YashaYahu / Is. 58).

RELIGION OF TRADITIONS
MEN'S TEACHINGS TURNED ASIDE TO MYTHS

TORAH OR TRADITION?

"Love Me and keep My Commandments."
— Ex 20:6, Dt 5:10

Some are confused because they are taught the Ten Commandments are a curse, and done away by being nailed to the stake.

It was not the Commandments, but the **list of our crimes** nailed to the stake. Yahusha became our **cheirographon** (legal term for the list of accusations). He became sin for us, erasing all the words that stood against us. We are free, and in His power we live by every Word that proceeds from the mouth of Yahuah. He created us to love Him, and the Ten Commandments teach us how to love Him and our neighbor.

He created us to be His companions. We cannot expect to be lawless and at the same time be accepted. When we obey another instead, it hurts Him. He is jealous for our affection.

Nimrod's **religion of traditions** breaks the everlasting Covenant.

The Second Coming will wipe-clean the traditions and decisions of all the councils, and we will reboot to the Living Words of Yahuah only. Traditions are so anchored to family and cultural bonds that any attempt to meddle with them is useless. Yahusha will have to burn the world down to cure the illness. Yahusha's Natsarim don't use any sacraments, and Yahusha is our only teaching authority. Our behavior is vastly different from the fourth beast's **religion of traditions.**

The "traditions of the fathers" was the religion of the Pharisees, and was a very heavy yoke.

Yahusha's yoke is light, but men have rejected it and invented their own yoke of human traditions in its place. Most have no idea how far they have fallen away from the Truth.

Natsarim are the repairers of the breach. We teach the Commandments as written in order to shape hearts with Yahuah's will; love is the outcome. Yahusha is in charge at all times, and no one gets burned, hung, or judged; He is the only Judge.

We work among those who serve the religion of traditions, but we don't observe those traditions.

We are free, because we abide in Yahuah's Word, not man's.

We cast down strongholds and all false reasoning with the Truth, in love. Yahusha's yoke sets us free.

Religion is **tradition**; but knowing the will of Yahusha is **reality**. The fruits of His Spirit are evident.

The words of all the councils will pass away, but Yahusha's Words will never pass away. When we live by every Word that proceeds from the mouth of Yahuah, the yoke of men's teachings are lifted from our shoulders.

We cannot serve both Yahuah and men's teachings.

If we abide in Yahusha, we will know the Truth, and the Truth will free us from men's traditions.

The mother of harlots is the pattern of

The Invisible Beast
The golden cup of Babel has caused madness.

The mark of this unrecognized beast is painless, until you awaken to it and resist it, showing you are not in compliance with the old fertility habits handed-down over many generations.

These customs are exoterically invisible to the uninitiated, but esoterically, blatantly obvious.

Every merchant prospers from the fertility celebrations that hardly anyone perceives because they are all hypnotized from a lifetime of exposure to the traditions handed-down from our fathers to children.

Idolatry is exactly what Yahusha referred to as stumbling blocks at Mt. 18:3-8. Idolatry is taught to children, and passes into each new generation through family bonding. Yahuah is sending the plagues now, but most people don't know why. Revelation 9:20:

"And the rest of mankind, who were not killed by these plagues, did not repent of the works of their hands, that they should not worship the demons, and idols of gold, and of silver, and of brass, and of stone, and of wood, which are neither able to see, nor to hear, nor to walk."

Merchants reinforce the wormwood-trance that caused the madness, and the masses remain in a drunken stupor. They are captives, enslaved by the idolatrous fertility traditions.

BUYERS & SELLERS OF IDOLATRY

Accepting the mark of this *unrecognized beast* is painless, until you awaken to it and resist it, showing you are not in compliance with the old fertility habits handed-down over many generations. By withholding your participation in the idolatry, your family takes an immediate interest in how you suddenly became *different*. They feel you are shunning them, but it's the culture everyone is embedded in that is making you stand away from their party invitations.

They wonder why you no longer run into the same **idolatrous behavior** you once practiced, although in ignorance. Peter mentions the indecencies, calling them **abominable idolatry**:

"For we have spent enough of our past lifetime in doing the desire of the nations, walking in indecencies, lusts, drunkenness, orgies, wild parties, and abominable idolatries, in which they are surprised that you do not run with them in the same flood of loose behavior, blaspheming, who shall give an account to Him who is ready to judge the living and the dead." 1 Peter / Kefa 4:3-5

The merchants promote all the trappings well in advance to the crowds to propel them headlong into mindless debt while never asking, *Why?* They are programmed to celebrate each fertility festival in its time, showing their children, parents, relatives, employers, teachers, and friends, how well they unknowingly serve the system, an ***unrecognized beast***, over all of humanity.

Read these Scriptures: MatithYahu 15:9, 1 Peter 4, Romans 1, Revelation 9, Revelation 18, & Mal. 4.

The woman riding (directing) the beast with all the fertility practices is teaching the masses all the arrogant nonsense:

"And the light of a lamp shall not shine in you any more at all. And the voice of bridegroom and bride shall not be heard in you any more at all. For your merchants were the great ones of the arets [Earth]**, for by your drug sorcery all the nations were led astray."** Rev. 18:23

Idolatry is accepted by all, and mostly unrecognized

(invisible) because it is unchallenged by teachers. They leave it alone, never going near it, like the third-rail of a subway train track; it would destroy their finances if they disputed it. If they let any hint of Truth out, revealing the devil's schemes behind traditions, their authority to teach their denomination's lies would be revoked.

They only teach worthless, futile traditions.
The lies are undetected when the teachers fail to teach Yahuah's Word, so the devil gets away with deceiving the whole World (Rev. 12). The teachers grant authority to teach their uncontested lies under the disguise of **dispensationalism**, **replacement theology**, and **denominations** named by men, and cause millions to live by all the ancient practices Yahuah hates.

The great number of teachers are given credibility by one another to prevail over the people, deciding who is to teach, and what to teach.

They encourage idolatry, teaching small bits of Yahuah's Word by snatching a little from here, and a little from there. (This relates to YashaYahu / Is. 28:10) Everything taught involves proof-texting, hunting for what they *already believe*, a teaching method known as *eisegesis*. Words and phrases become *triggers*, and people are programmed to recall only what they have been taught when they hear a word or phrase. The people are fed **wormwood** because teachers have twisted Yahuah's Words, and this numbs their senses. They make *pagan* stuff mean *other* stuff, conquering the unquestioning minds of the gullible. They are all **Nicolaitanes** (Rev 2), a word meaning **conquerors of the people**. The laity is the lowest of the 3 estates: ***clergy, nobility, & laity.***

Syncretism conceals the idolatry under a disguise, making stuff seem to mean other stuff. They confuse, alter, and excuse the witchcraft by compromising everything with ideas outside of Yahuah's Word.

Are Halloween, Christmas, & Easter Concealing Anything?

Yes, they're obviously heathen, and pastors have not warned us. Babel's esoteric **Easter** (Ishtar) uses rabbits and eggs (fertility symbols) to associate with Yahusha's resurrection. This is *syncretism*, and so is Christmas, the rebirth of the Sun deity (King Nimrod, aka satan). Yahusha pitched His tent, or tabernacled among men during *Sukkoth*.

There is **nothing** celebrated by Christians that aligns with Scripture, and the behavior of Yahusha, or His Natsarim. Sun-day, Halloween, Christmas, and Easter are all habits our fathers have inherited from heathen Sun worshipers, and these things are why the inhabitants of the Earth are to be burned on the **Day of Yahuah** (YashaYahu 24, Mt. 24, Yual / Joel 2, Malaki 4). **fossilizedcustoms.com/christmas.html**

On Halloween, we place a sign on our door declaring *"No Candy Here,"* and it explains how Halloween is idolatry, with Scripture references Mt. 18, 1 Peter 4, Ephesians 2, Dt. 12, & Jer. 10 (See More Resources). Romans 6 explains why we cannot participate in such idolatry. On this same "Halloween poster," Goliath has his Easter basket, and young is David winding-up his sling to put a stone into his brain. Yahuah's *Name* is often referred to as a *stone*, and the builders rejected it.

NO CANDY HERE

HAVE YOU NOT HEARD?

HALLOWEEN

IS IDOLATRY

BASED ON NECROMANCY

ROMANS 6
MT. 18, 1 PETER 4, EPHESIANS 2, MAL. 4, DT. 12, JER. 10

YAHUSHA IS COMING SOON

AND HIS REWARD IS WITH HIM

502.261.9833

UNCONDITIONAL LOVE?

Teachers say the love of Yahuah is unconditional, the Torah is done-away, and obedience is unnecessary, just believe. But, they do not know Yahuah, nor His Name! 1 Yn. 2:4 proves this. If they say *"I know Him,"* but do not guard His Commandments, they are liars, and the Truth is not in them.

"Do not learn the way of the gentiles" (YirmeYahu / Jer. 10:2) means exactly what it says.
The Galatians were converts from the ways of the gentiles, and Paul asked them if he had become their enemy because he told them the Truth. - See Gal. 4:16

Sun-day is not the Sun's day, nor is it a day of rest. It's the first day of the week, *day one.*

The world uses pagan names for some of their months, and the days of the week, but we use the number instead. When talking to someone who is unaware, I'll often describe it this way:

"on the 4th day, the one that most people think begins with the letter double-u, . . ."

As they pause a moment to work that out in their mind, I may add:

"I don't call days or months by the names of pagan idols, that would be illegal."

When my wife and I read Ex. 23:13 we understood what Yahuah meant, and we raised our children to learn to love Yahuah by doing what is *pleasing in His sight.* May Yahuah continue to teach us all, and bless and guard us as we learn from Him.

YashaYahu / Isaiah 6:5 expresses the prophet's anguish as he recognized how truly set-apart Yahuah is, and how filthy he was as he lived among people with unclean lips. The prophet said, ***"I am undone!"*** We have to think carefully before we open our mouth to speak. We have to turn over all control to Yahuah. Ps. 19:14 is a prayer that pertains not only to what we say, but what is in our hearts. Yahuah knows all, even the motivation behind what we say and do.

We want to please, serve, and obey Yahuah no matter the cost. What others my think of us is of no concern. YashaYahu 51:7 is another text to radically accept the will of Yahuah. Yahusha wants us to be hot, not lukewarm. He knows if we're really His, and when He knows it, we know it, and everyone around us knows it. For this, we are hated as they hated Him. We are either salt, or we're not.

What A Difference A Day Makes
The Norse greatly influenced the language of those living in Angle Land (England).

Odin / Woden gives the world the word "Wednes' (Woden's) Day." The world worships demons, and they reinforce their control over us by simply using these false names. Woden represents the Sun deity, Nimrod, among the babbled languages. The word Odin traces back to Adun / Adon, a word meaning *LORD* in Eberith / Hebrew.

Order Fossilized Customs for more details

WEEKDAYS - IDOLS' NAMES

What evidence can be shown to a deluded person who may want proof that idolatry has captured the collective consciousness of all mankind?

The names used for the days of the week show just how prominent idolatry is, and how it goes **undetected**. How is it possible so few have noticed?

SUNDAY

The day of the Sun (dies Solis), excused as the *LORD's Day.* In Hindi, the same day of the week is called **Ravi vara**, named this to honor their **Sun** deity, Surya. The term Ravivara means LORD's Day.

MONDAY

The day of the Moon

TUESDAY

The day of Tyr, a Norse deity, from the proto Indo-European word deya, *to shine.*

WEDNESDAY

Woden's day, or Odin's daeg. This was the Norse Sun deity whose symbol was the Celtic crux, used widely by many circuses today. It's a cross with a solar circle around the point of intersection.

To Constantine, it would be Apollo, and to Babylonians, it would be Shammash Nimrod, the Sun.

THURSDAY
Thor's Day, the Norse deity of thunder. Druid priests and other pagans know his symbol is a T-shape, or hammer.

FRIDAY
The day of Frigga, wife of Woden. In Norse tradition, her symbol is the fish.
Fish are known to produce high numbers of eggs, so she is a fertility deity.

SATURDAY - SEVENTH DAY
The day of Saturnus, a roman deity.
(See more in Fossilized Customs 12th ed.)

OPINION OF HABIT
"Men like the opinions to which they have been accustomed from their youth; they defend them, and shun contrary views; and this is one of the things that prevents men from finding truth, for they cling to the opinion of habit." - quoted from Guide For The Perplexed, Maimonides (1135-1204)

Do We Become Unclean Each Time We Touch A Dead Animal?
It depends on whether or not the dead animal is clean or unclean (Lev. 11). Touching a human dead body, or the carcass of any unclean animal, causes us to be unclean temporarily. After we bath and change our clothing, we are unclean until evening, which begins a new day. YashaYahu 66:15-17 predicts the fiery end for those who eat the flesh of pigs, rats, or any other abominations on the Day of Yahuah.
We can touch the body of LIVING unclean animals, but certainly we cannot eat their carcasses. Petting your cat or dog is fine, but don't stuff a dead pet and

keep it lying around your home. Tiger rugs or rhino heads hanging on the wall are also not things we would have any business owning, or even being in any room with. Most people don't know it, but the *"genuine cowhide leather"* scriptures are repurposed pigskins processed to appear to be cowhide.

Our Deluxe Cover BYNV translation uses a polyurethane (PU), an imitation leather.

Our teachers have led us away from sound teaching. Psalm 1 tells us what makes the difference between a green tree, and a dead one.

BIRTHDAY CELEBRATIONS

December 25th has been celebrated as the Sun's birthday for over 4000 years. It was adopted as the nativity of Yahusha. They concealed Yahusha's Name by using the christogram **IESV** to encrypt His real Name. *The masses have embraced a false name as well as false worship, and they live on wormwood fed to them by their teachers.*

Nimrod was the first human being to be worshipped as the Sun, and the basis for the Sun's birthday to occur at the winter Solstice. After Yahuah foiled Nimrod's plan to build the Tower of Babel by confusing all the languages, Sun worshippers fumbled to say Nimrod. The Sun deity became known in all kinds of *babbled* forms: Shammash, Mithras, Molok, Baal, Apollo, Helios, Krishna, Surya, and all the rest. They are all worshipping satan. Read Malaki 4:1-6, and it will make you ask yourself how they tricked you for so long, and why they have not warned anyone. These things being discussed are only the foothills of a huge conspiracy to control teachings.

Tradition has caused Nimrod's *secret identity* to become even more obscured. The modern world calls him **Santa**. Secretly, *Santa is Nimrod.*

IS SANTA SATAN?
video link: **https://youtu.be/WVcajZAY6lc**
Satan is the "**father of lies**."
He is also known as "**Old Nick**."
Due to the *babbling lips* caused by Nimrod's rebellion, the modern Santa character has been able to conceal that Nimrod and Santa are the same.
The powers in the heavenlies arrayed against us have programmed us to lie to our own children, deceiving them to believe in a lie. Children are the openly targeted audience in all the idolatrous pagan activities we see everywhere around us. They are unwittingly honoring the *king of Babel.*
Nimrod is the ancient **serpent king** seeking to be like Yahuah, portrayed in the logo of *Superman*, a serpent on his chest depicting a serpent.

Satan gets no push-back from Christian pastors. YashaYahu 14:12-21 describes the fallen one as the "king of Babel."
"How you are fallen from heaven Helel Ben Shakar, son of the morning! How you are cut down to the ground, you who weakened the nations!
For you have said in your heart: 'I will ascend into heaven,
I will exalt my THRONE above the stars of Alahim;

I will also sit on the mount of the assembly on the farthest sides of the <u>NORTH</u>; I will ascend above the heights of the clouds; I will be like the Most High.' Yet you shall be brought down to Sheol, to the lowest depths of the Pit. Those who see you will gaze at you, and consider you, saying:
'Is this the man who made the earth tremble, who shook kingdoms, who made the world as a wilderness and destroyed its cities, who did not open the house of his prisoners?'
All the kings of the nations, all of them, sleep in esteem, everyone in his own house; but you are cast out of your grave like an abominable branch, like the garment of those who are slain, thrust through with a sword, who go down to the stones of the pit, like a corpse trodden underfoot. You will not be joined with them in burial, because you have destroyed your land and slain your people.
The brood of evildoers shall never be named. Prepare slaughter for his children because of the iniquity of their fathers, lest they rise up and possess the land, and fill the face of the world with cities."

Satan, Superman, Nimrod, and all the Sun deities of the nations, are all the same person: the king of Babel described above.

How Our Minds Were Opened By Yahusha

Malaki 4:1-6 explains the reason the fire is coming upon the disobedient. One of the first questions my wife and I asked over 35 years ago was *"what are we supposed to obey?"* The pastor didn't have a specific answer, so we turned to the Word of Yahuah, and we found it. We have to be careful how we listen; the traditions are men's teachings; but the Ten Commandments are forever. Eccl. 12:13-14 says they are for all mankind to obey. Somehow, we heard the Word, and now we love obedience. Why not try it, and see if it is good, or bad? Where can we find them, across the sea? They've been with us all along, but men's teachings have kept them from us. They say, "swerve from that path!" YashaYahu 51:7 says, "Listen to Me, you who know obedience, a people in whose heart is My Torah; do not fear the reproach of mere mortals, nor listen to their insults!"

A Book That's Scarier Than Halloween
Yahuah's first month of His year is in the spring, see Exodus 12:2. Yahuah's appointed times foreshadow His overall redemption plan.

The arrival of the 7th month each year (not Rome's reckoning, but Yahuah's) are the last unfulfilled shadows of His redemption plan. The first day of the seventh month is Yom Teruah, or day of the shout. On the Day of Yahuah, the tenth day of the 7th month, is our FAST (Acts 27:9). When fulfilled, malakim will remove all unsealed inhabitants from the Earth. The reapers (eagles, seraphim) will burn the weeds first, then gather the wheat into the new Yerushalim coming down from the skies. None of this is "Jewish," or limited to only regathering one tribe. Yahusha is coming back to His treasured possession, His inheritance - those who are waiting for Him. He's staying to reign with them right here for 1000 years. Most people are expecting a completely different outcome. We will not see Him again until we say, ***Baruk haba baShem Yahuah!"***
(Luke 19:38-40, Psalm 118:26)

Scarier Day Than Halloween
video link: **https://youtu.be/fAV4Wdx-NBU**
A warning message from the last Natsarim about how the way of Truth has been maligned: Christianity absorbed the ways of the gentiles who were unconverted heathens. Re-inventing the customs of Babel and modeling their practices according to Druids will cost billions of people dearly. Steeples and Sunday worshippers will not survive the return of Yahusha. *Turning aside to myths happens; what could possibly go wrong?*

When Does A Day Begin?
Muslims start their day at sunrise, the Romans at midnight. What do we see written in the Word of Yahuah, our model to live by?
"There was *evening*, and there was *morning*, the first day." Barashith / Genesis 1:5
Evening begins a new day, and this is confirmed by many examples in Scripture. At Exodus 12, we read: "From the *evening* of the fourteenth day of the first month to the *evening* of the 21st day, you must not eat any bread made with yeast."
They were told to eat the lamb inside, and not to go outside until morning.
The lamb was not eaten at breakfast, but eaten during darkness.
The messenger of Yahuah went out that same night to kill all the firstborn of men and animals.
Yahusha died late in the day on the 14th of the 1st month, a preparation day for Matsah. They hurried to take Yahusha's body down from the stake before sunset because the first day of Matsah was arriving (Yn. 19:31). Yom Kafar is a 24-hour period of fasting, and from *"evening-to-evening."* see Lev. 23:32

The *Quranic day* begins in the morning, the *Roman* day begins at midnight, but we Natsarim begin our day at <u>sunset</u>.

Some Teachers Say A Day Begins At Sunrise.
Why Do So Many Scriptures Say Something Else?
The Scriptures of Truth guide us by using context to explain Yahuah's intended meaning of His words. In trying to understand when a "day" begins, we look at how Yahuah explains it, knowing He knows, and some of us may not.
We know Unleavened Bread is for seven "days." When those seven "days" begin and end are very easy to see: "In the first month you are to eat unleavened bread, from the evening of the fourteenth day until the evening of the twenty-first day. For seven days there must be no leaven found in your houses." - (Exodus 12:18-19). There is no wiggle room left when we surrender to obedience and remove the excuses men have invented to cause divisions. When we obey the instructions as written, Yahusha refines us further. If we resist, the understanding we think we possess will be taken away from us. Read the book, The LIE - look inside the book at amazon, Lew White's author's page.

Also see this webpage for further study on when a day begins:
fossilizedcustoms.com/day.html

DAY Can Mean More Than One Thing
Observing a DAY as *evening-to-evening* is being challenged by *morning-to-morning* teachings.
The Quranic DAY begins in the morning, and a Roman DAY at midnight, but what does the Scripture of Truth teach us? The problem is bound-up in the limited meaning some have assigned to the word

day. The highly-flexible word YOM is often lost in translation. Their context gives us the proper sense of what words mean. The seven DAYS of Matsah commence and end in the evening:

Exo 12:15: *"'Seven DAYS you shall eat unleavened bread. Indeed on the first DAY you cause leaven to cease from your houses. For whoever eats leavened bread from the first DAY until the seventh DAY, that being shall be cut off from Yisharal.'"*

Exo 12:18: *"'In the first month, on the fourteenth DAY of the month, in the evening, you shall eat unleavened bread until the twenty-first DAY of the month in the evening.'"*

Counting the 7 days on your fingers, you see that it begins at the end of the 14th day in the evening, and extends to the 21st day in the evening.

Seven DAYS of Matsah commence and end in the evening, and so does Yom Kafar (DAY of atonement in the seventh month).

Danial 8 mentions 2300 evenings and mornings. Notice these two verses in the book of Acts:

Act 27:27: *"And when the fourteenth NIGHT came, as we were driven up and down in the Adriatic Sea, about midnight the sailors suspected that they were drawing near some land."*

Act 27:33: *"And when DAY was about to come, Paul urged them all to take food, saying, 'Today is the fourteenth DAY you have continued without food, and eaten none at all.'"*

There was evening, and there was morning, the first DAY; a day begins with evening, and at evening a new DAY begins.

THE GARDENER

The Festivals of Yahuah are appointments He gave us during the year (Lev. 23 & Dt. 16). He says they are His appointments, and His people are to observe them and teach them. They are shadowy outlines He guides us in to follow His redemption plan, and are for all who join to Him. They are an outline (shadow, model) of things to come for the body of Yahusha. By observing His work of redemption, we see His purpose is to grow mankind so His Life (living waters) can flow throughout His garden to bear His fruit in the branches.

He uses agricultural metaphors (ideal gardening practices) to illustrate the appointed times so we can grow to become workers in His Garden. The Gardener looks for good fruit, and His harvesters will not harm those who have His seal (Name) marking them as His property. Without obedience, it is impossible to please Him, or be capable of producing good fruit. An enemy has sown tares among the wheat, and they grow together until the time of the harvest. The reapers will go forth on His order at an appointed time, and remove the tares first, and burn them. Then, those same reapers will gather the wheat into the barn (sukkah) at the marriage supper of the Lamb.

As we learn and observe the times, we do our best to obey the instructions given for each one of them. We can't do anything to redeem ourselves, however if the appointed times says to rest, we rest from doing servile work on those days. Yom Kafar (10th day of 7th month) is a Shabath of Shabathuth - and we afflict our beings (it's *the Fast*, Acts 27:9).

The Fast on Yom Kafar

We afflict our beings by doing without food from sunset on the 9th to sunset on the 10th (of the 7th month). This is not a thought process like the Greek mindset would have us believe, but an actual fast (see Acts 27:9). The idea is not to make ourselves sick, so take a little water to help.

You won't feel the hunger until late afternoon, and that's when we really pay attention to the strength Yahusha gives us to overcome our flesh.

After you get through one, you will see how our flesh tries to rule our minds under normal day-to-day conditions, but this ought not to be the case.

Our flesh cannot be allowed to boss us around!

The FAST (Acts 27:9) teaches us to rely on overcoming the flesh in the power of the Ruach. We learn how to reduce selfish impulses, and share our blessings with those who desperately need what we have in abundance. The teaching Yahusha gives at Luke 16:19-31 shows us His perspective of how our selfish behavior impacts others. Each choice we make to withhold from the needy, who live all around us, will have consequences both in the present and the future.

A TRUE FAST

"Cry aloud, do not spare. Lift up your voice like a ram's horn. Declare to My people their transgression, and the house of Yaqub their sins. Yet they seek Me yom by yom, and delight to know My ways, as a nation that did obedience, and did not forsake the lawfulness of their Alahim.

*They ask of Me rulings of obedience, they delight
in drawing near to Alahim. They say, 'Why have
we fasted, and You have not seen?*
*Why have we afflicted our beings, and You took
no note?' Look, in the yom of your fasting you
find pleasure, and drive on all your laborers.
Look, you fast for strife and contention, and to
strike with the fist of lawlessness.*
*You do not fast as you do this yom, to make your
voice heard on high.*
*Is it a fast that I have chosen, a yom for a man to
afflict his being? Is it to bow down his head like a
bulrush, and to spread out sackcloth and ashes?
Do you call this a fast, and an acceptable yom to
Yahuah? Is this not the fast that I have chosen: to
loosen the tight cords of lawlessness, to undo
the bands of the yoke, to exempt the oppressed,
and to break off every*
*yoke? Is it not to share your bread with the
hungry, and that you bring to your house the
poor who are cast out; when you see the naked,
and cover him, and not hide yourself from your
own flesh? Then your light would break forth like
the morning, your healing spring forth speedily.
And your obedience shall go before you, the
esteem of Yahuah would be your rear guard.
Then, when you call, Yahuah would answer;
when you cry, He would say, 'Here I am.' If you
take away the yoke from your midst, the pointing
of the finger, and the speaking of disobedience, if
you extend your being to the hungry and satisfy
the afflicted being, then your light shall dawn in
the darkness, and your darkness be as noon.
Then Yahuah would guide you continually, and
satisfy your being in drought, and strengthen*

your bones. And you shall be like a watered garden, and like a spring of water, whose mayim do not fail. And those from among you shall build the old ruins. You shall raise up the foundations of many generations. And you would be called the Repairer of the Break, the Restorer of Streets to Dwell In. If you do turn back your foot from the Shabath, from doing your pleasure on My qodesh yom, and shall call the Shabath a delight, the qodesh yom of Yahuah esteemed, and shall esteem it, not doing your own ways, nor finding your own pleasure, nor speaking your own words, then you shall delight yourself in Yahuah. And I shall cause you to ride on the heights of the arets, and feed you with the inheritance of Yaqub your father. For the mouth of Yahuah has spoken!" - YashaYahu / Isaiah 58:1-14

The weekly day of rest (Shabath) is the sign of the eternal Covenant, and we follow the instructions given in the 4th Commandment. It is the 7th day of each week that Yahuah started at Creation week. The week (SHABUA) is a repeating cycle of 7 days. The annual "high" days are observed beginning in the spring. They begin in the first month of the year (Exodus 12:2).

Domes, holy water, beads, circumambulation, and crescents are foreign to Yahuah and will *disappear* on the day of our redemption.

200 BCE: THE SILK ROAD BROUGHT SHIVA WORSHIP TO THE MIDDLE EAST

Origins Of The Crescent Symbol

A *sighted-moon* is not found in the Scriptures of Truth, but rather the practice is an Islamic pattern adopted by the first Karaite, "rabbi" Anan (767 CE). Islam adopted the symbol of the crescent from Hinduism's symbol of Shiva. The Silk Road trade route brought many practices into the Middle East when India's borders swelled in 200 BCE.

The Karaites observe Bikkurim correctly, as it is always on the first day of the week, but their **crescent-sighting** is how their founder's life was spared. Detailed research will prove this, but this tradition of sighting crescents is not in Scripture. **fossilizedcustoms.com/sightedmoonorigins.html**

Domes, holy water, beads, circumambulation, and crescents are foreign to Yahuah and will disappear on the day of our redemption.

THE PATH TO TRUTH

The path to Truth involves trusting Yahuah's Word, and forgiving those who have offended us. We need to submit to being shaped by what was intended for evil, and letting Yahuah turn it into a blessing. Yahusha's indwelling gives us the power to overcome strongholds (false ideas), and surrender to the Truth and hold it fast.

We soon realize only Yahusha can guide us, not a teaching authority that presents itself with titles and credentials. These only lead us away from Yahusha, because they are false shepherds. Labels are another divisive approach we can fall into. Some may misunderstand us when we say *"like the Jews did"* - as if to imply all Yahudim then (and now) are in the same boat, deceived and being deceived - which is not true.

It was the **teaching authority** (then and now) that is confusing people. When we reject the human teachers with all their traditions (leaven), and study the Word of Yahuah for ourselves as we should, then the veil is lifted and our true Shepherd reveals His will to us. His purpose for us is different than the false shepherds, which is why the false shepherds are so disturbed by our rejection of them. By their fruits, you will discern them.

Our confusion stems from the traditions we've inherited from our forefathers. Remember, as mentioned earlier, Maimonides wrote:

"Men like the opinions to which they have been accustomed from their youth; they defend them, and shun contrary views; and this is one of the things that prevents men from finding truth, for they cling to the opinion of habit."
- *Guide For The Perplexed*

Human traditions are the most insidious enemy of the Truth. When a lie is discovered, immediately the truth-bearer is maligned as the evil one, and compromises begin to form in order to preserve tradition.

GOD: IS THIS THE NAME OF OUR CREATOR?
Exodus 23:13 prohibits us from taking the names of Pagan deities on our lips. With that in mind, the origin of the term *GOD* will exempt it from our use. The 1945 Encyclopedia Americana has this to say under to topic GOD:

"GOD (god) Common Teutonic word for personal object of religious worship, formerly applicable to super-human beings of heathen myth; on conversion of Teutonic races to Christianity, term was applied to Supreme Being."

Nimrod is the basis of the Epic of Gilgamesh, and familiar names like Apollo, Zeus, Ra, Krishna, Mithras, and all other mythological Sun deities. The myths originate from the idea that Nimrod became the Sun.

The worship of the *host of heaven* (astrology) is still infecting the minds of the young and old. All Sun deities' births are celebrated on December 25. Without knowing it, people are now referring to Nimrod by the name "Santa." Much more detail about this may be discovered in another book, **Nimrod's Secret Identity** (available at amazon as an eBook or printed).

SIGNS & WONDERS
Some are looking for a sign before they decide between the fake name JESUS and the one true Name YAHUSHA. Jesuits invented the name JESUS less than 500 years ago; Mushah changed the name of HUSHA to YAHUSHA over 3300 years ago. (See interlinear text at Numbers 13:16)

Signs and wonders are for *unbelievers*, please read 1 Korinthians 14:20-22. There are other texts related to this idea, such as Mt. 16:4:

"A wicked and adulterous generation seeks for a sign, but none will be given except the sign of Yunah."

The teaching of the name JESUS is not yet 500 years old, so it is the false name. Look to the Eberith script, perhaps beginning with the interlinear text at ZekarYah 3; they transliterate YAHUSHA as JOSHUA, but the Aramith letters prove the letter "J" is false, and the name it is attached to. There can be only one (Acts 4:12) by which we must be delivered.

THE IMPOSTER

A fake name the world has been trained to accept is JESUS CHRIST. This name is less than 500 years old, and is a promotion of the Jesuits (Societas IESU, or Society of Jesus). Rather than using Hebrew, it uses Greek and Latin, in place of the true (and only) Hebrew Name of the Mashiak, **Yahusha** (translated, "I am your Deliverer").

The true Name can be seen in the Hebrew text at ZekarYah 3. Other forms of it in transliterated form include **Yahushua** (seen 2 times), and a shortened form, **Y'shua**, which is found *one time* at Numbers 13:12.

JESUS means nothing in *Hebrew*, the language from which we are barred from expressing the true Name, *Yahusha*. JESUS cannot be transliterated back to Hebrew and maintain the original sound or character of the true Name. *JESUS* is derived from the Greek letters *IESOU*. This was transliterated from a Hebrew acronym, **YESHU**, standing for *yemak-shemu-uzikro*, meaning *"may his name and memory be destroyed."* This is a long-standing curse spoken by the unbelieving authorities within Rabbinic Judaism. Some believe, or may later, so be careful what you say and think in your heart about anyone.

The closest-sounding Hebrew name to IESU is ESU (Esau, ayin-shin-uau, meaning "hairy"). After we scrape the dirt away, a precious Pearl of great value will be found; don't stop digging for it.

fossilizedcustoms.com/iesu.html

Baruk Haba BaShem Yahuah

We, Yahusha's Natsarim, need to be forgiving and compassionate to those who spread malicious gossip about us. Acts 28:22 says our sect is spoken against everywhere.

Yahusha is refining each of us to be useful examples of His character to those we interact with every day. 2 Peter 1:3-7 tells us that Yahusha helps us reflect His virtues and behavior in order to be effective examples of Himself. His work in us builds-up others, and draws the lost to Him through our own good behavior.

Keep the lost and all the Natsarim in constant prayer, especially during these times of great distress. Cities are burning, and the dragon is unleashing his worst.

BARUK HABA BASHEM YAHUAH (Google it).

FINGER OF YAHUAH
Yahusha Wrote Something In The Dust

The names of those who depart from Yahuah's Torah are written in the Earth, and blow away like dust. YirmeYahu / Jer. 17:13 says, ***"Those who depart from Me shall be written in the arets*** [Earth] ***because they have forsaken Yahuah, the fountain of living mayim."***

Let's consider what Yahusha wrote in the dust at the time the woman was brought before Him at Yahukanon / John chapter 8. Some strongly believe it was the names of the men demanding Him to give His opinion: ***to stone her, or let her live.***

They asked Him what needed to be done to the woman caught in the act of breaking wedlock; but they did so with the motive to entrap <u>*Him*</u>. Yahusha knew this.

What Yahusha wrote in the dust in front of the men compelled them not only to pause, but to *walk away* – beginning with those who were the oldest.

Of the 10 Commandments He'd written in stone with His finger, the 7th was likely what Yahusha re-wrote in the dust. This would define the sin of breaking the vow of wedlock, and not to violate it. It requires only a few letters.

LA TENAF is the transliteration of 6 Hebrew letters found twice in Scripture, Ex. 20:14 & Dt. 5:18. Dt. 22:22 prescribes *death* for <u>both</u> the *man* and the *woman* caught violating wedlock:

"When a man is found lying with a ashah married to a husband, then both of them shall die, both the man that lay with the ashah, and the ashah. Thus you shall purge the evil from Yisharal."

Standing up, Yahusha made a reply they did not expect:

"But as they kept on questioning Him, He straightened up and said to them, 'He who is without sin among you, let him be the first to throw a stone at her.' [next, Yahusha writes *more*] **And bending down again, He wrote on the ground.**

And when they heard it, being reproved by their conscience, went out one by one, beginning from the older ones until the last." -Yn. 8:7-9 BYNV

They were caught in their own trap, because Yahusha wrote the **name of the man** involved. They would have read it with great interest, seeing the name of their fellow conspirator next to the 7th Commandment.

It was the *second time* He bent down to write the name of the man, and their behavior shows how deeply involved in the plot every one of the men were.

Who Were These Accusers, And Where Was The Man?

At Yn. / Jn. 8:7-9, who were the men sent to trap Yahusha on a point of the law concerning the woman caught in the very act of breaking wedlock, yet failed to bring along the man she was caught with?

The men were most likely sent by, or even members of, the *Sanhedrin*.

They were attempting to entrap Yahusha. The fact that they planned to execute someone on a point of the law shows a high level of contempt for the things He was teaching every day, and they wanted to expose *Him* as a lawbreaker.

"And Yahusha straightening up and seeing no one but the ashah said to her, 'Ashah, where are those accusers of yours? Did no one condemn you?' And she said, 'No one Master.' And Yahusha said to her, 'Neither do I condemn you. Go and sin no more.' - Yn. 8:10-11

CONSPIRATORS TERRIFIED

The accusers had plotted far more than discrediting Yahusha; they wanted to kill Him as well as the woman. It's easy to see *why the man caught in the act with the woman* was not brought forth. The man was obviously involved in the plot, and the man did not want his name to come out in the open. Yahusha knows all secrets, and He knew the name of the man, and all those involved in the conspiracy. The man's name must have been the name Yahusha wrote in the dust.

This would have been more than enough to terrify them all.

Yahusha didn't have to write very much in the dust to turn them on their heels. Who would want to hang around to watch Him write *their* name down?

"The Word of Yahuah is living, and working, and sharper than any two-edged sword, cutting through even to the dividing of being and ruach, and of joints and marrow, and able to judge the thoughts and intentions of the heart.
And there is no creature hidden from His sight, but all are naked and laid bare before the eyes of Him with whom is our account. Therefore, since we have a great High Priest who has passed

through the shamayim, Yahusha the Son of Yahuah, let us hold fast our admission.
For we do not have a High Priest unable to sympathize with our weaknesses, but One who was tested in all respects as we are, apart from sin. Therefore, let us come boldly to the throne of favor, in order to receive compassion, and find favor for timely help." Hebrews 4:12-16

The One Who gave us His Turah is the only One Who can forgive transgressions, and that was the outcome in this circumstance.

Yahusha showed How kind He can be to **all** of us sinners, if we turn from sin. All He asks of us is to stop sinning, and love Him by obeying His Commandments.

Sinners have hope in Yahusha because He comprehends our weaknesses, and gives us strength to overcome them by His indwelling. He is the Helper living in all those who are His, and He will never leave us. He is the Way, the Truth, and the Life, and He loves us.

The world has been listening to men saying that some, or all, of the Ten Commandments were annulled, in spite of Yahusha's words at Mt. 5:19. The Turah has fallen in the streets, and has been trampled underfoot by men (Is. 59:14, Mt. 5:13). The blood of Yahusha made *one* offering for sin, *replacing* the old priesthood (Heb. 8:13). The renewed Covenant is remembered at Pesak (Passover) as Yahusha said to remember it. The new priesthood and High Priest made the old covenant *obsolete*. The old covenant was not the Ten Words written by the finger of Yahuah, but rather was written on a sefer (vellum, *gebel*, an animal hide) to direct animal blood-offerings for sin.

It was that *old covenant* He was referring to when He said *"Shalom"* from the stake in His last breath. Yahusha's blood completely and permanently redeems us if we trust in it, and not the *blood of animals.*

The eternal Covenant in the stone tablets is thought to be impossible to obey by the false teaching authorities, yet it's easy. They desire to become teachers, yet forsake Turah. Look at Dt. 31:26, and you'll see the word *scroll*; Yahuah ordered it placed BESIDE the ark. YirmeYahu [Jer.] 31:31-34 refers to the Covenant INSIDE the ark, and it will never fade or become obsolete. The hand written scroll that was added due to transgressions has now disappeared, along with the offerings of animal blood, the priesthood that conducted the operations, and the Temple where the blood of animals was offered. Some teachers say they've found the ark, but Revelation 11:19 says Yahuah has the ark of the Covenant in His possession.

Why Re-build A Temple?
Yahusha explained to the girl at Yn. 4 a time was coming when neither in that mountain nor in Yerushalim would true worshipers worship Abba. Why would anyone want to build a 3rd Temple to offer animal blood, and walk into an empty chamber to find no ark? Would it not be futility?
All the blood of the animals in the world could not redeem anyone at all.

"Unless Yahuah builds the house, the builders labor in vain." Psalm 127:1

The Bride of Yahusha Is The Ark
We are also the 3rd Temple, and He dwells in us.
I tell you a mystery - Kolossians 1:27.

The obedient ones are Yahusha's bride, and His inheritance, and He is our inheritance.

The time is coming when no one will ever think about the previous ark (Jer. 3:16).

For now, Yahusha's branches (Natsarim) are to teach the nations the Name of Yahuah, and to guard all He commanded us to guard, His Covenant of kindness. His bride is the reason He is coming back, she is His treasured possession.

He is not coming back to show us the Ark of the Covenant, but to indwell His living ark with His eternal Covenant, written in the hearts of those who love Him.

His bride is the ark, and His dwelling place. Without an ark, it's senseless futility to build a physical temple. The third temple is being built, and we who are teaching His Name and Word to the nations are spiritual stones. The Mind of the Ruach ha Qodesh is life and peace.

He is coming, and His reward is with Him.
The Spirit and the bride say, *"come."*
Revelation 22:17

Men's Philosophies Have Deceived Many

Men's philosophies still hold people in a thought prison (stronghold).

They think the Ten Commandments are the old covenant, and that Yahusha "did away" with them. The old covenant was written on a scroll, and directed the old priesthood to offer animal blood for temporary atonement. Yahusha ended that with one perfect offering of His Own blood for complete, permanent atonement for all who repent, call on His Name for the forgiveness of their sins, and obey His eternal Covenant now written on our hearts by His indwelling.

The falling-away from the walk in the extreme last days concerns the false teachings that direct people away from the eternal Covenant. This is what Kolossians 2:8, 2 Peter 2:2, and 3:15-17 are describing about those living today. The renewed Covenant is our trust in Yahusha's blood, not the old process, animal blood. His blood redeems us completely, doing away with the old priesthood, Temple, and offerings of animals' blood on the side of the ark by the former high priest. Yahusha came to destroy the works of the devil, not do away with His Commandments. Compare Dt. 31:26 and Hebrews 8:13. Note the old covenant was written on a scroll, and placed beside the ark - it is not the eternal marriage Covenant He wrote on the stone tablets. He has now written them on hearts (minds), and we receive a love for them, and we are sealed in His Name for the day of the redemption of our physical body. He has promised to cloth His obedient ones with immortality in the twinkling of an eye when He returns.

Planning A Rebuilt Temple
(with no Ark of the Covenant)?

Yn. 4:21 describes a *dwelling place* far different from what we see being planned for the Temple Mount, and not built with human hands. Would animal sacrifices starting-up again please Yahusha, or enrage Him? The animal blood and Temple services never redeemed anyone, being imperfect (the old covenant). They pointed toward the one perfect offering. Yahuah removed every stone built on the Temple Mount, and now we await His return, not a return to the old animal blood method. Some of us can imagine no greater insult to Yahusha than to set up animal sacrifices again, especially in the place where His Name dwells forever.

Did Yahusha say He is Lucifer?

Translators use words they inherited from traditional mistakes made before them.

Equivocating the king of Babel (YashaYahu 14:12) with the Ruler of the Universe, Yahusha (Revelation 22:16) is based on misinterpreting the word HILLEL (used one time, meaning shining). HILLEL BEN SHAKAR translates "shining son of morning," referring to the adversary who misled the nations in the worship of the host of heaven (zodiac nonsense). Yahusha - not JESUS - was speaking Eberith at Revelation 22:16, not Latin, nor did He claim His NAME was HA AUR (meaning *the light*).

He is *"the light of men,"* and guides us into all Truth. LUCIFER (Latin) means *light bearer.* Casuistry and equivocation are Jesuit skills (exercises) to deceptively make cases seem logical, but they are in fact designed to confuse. Check out this webpage: **fossilizedcustoms.com/casuistry.html**

WORDS CAN LEAD OR MISLEAD

The KJV is an Anglican Catholic translation from the Latin Vulgate into English. The first edition uses the IESV *(underlined)* as it appears in the Latin Vulgate. All that was known of the lights in the sky in the 17th century was based on the astrology they inherited from Babel. The book of Ayub (aka Job) describes starlight as AISH, infinity as KESIL, clusters of galaxies as KIMAH, and the whole collection of lights as MAZZAROTH. Proof-texting altered the meaning of these words, making them seem to be a bear and other animal - zoo collections people call the zodiac. The KJV removed the Name of Yahuah. It introduced the world to *the LORD,* and other translations have followed this pattern, calling it tradition. The message of AliYahu is in his name, and found at Malaki 4. How long will people sway between two opinions?

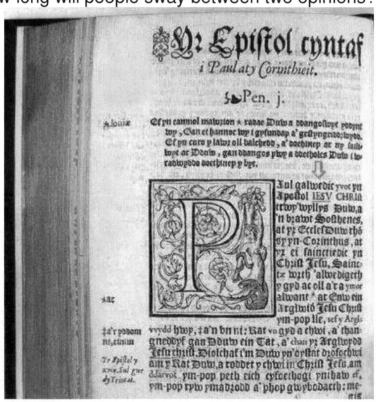

The first edition of the KJV shows the **IESV**.

Consider the word Vaticanus: The ancient Etruscan name for one of the seven hills of Rome.
The Etruscans and Romans used the area as a graveyard, and the area was very swampy. Today it is the location of Vatican City, adopting the name from the hill **Vaticanus**. In ancient Rome, the graves were shallow, dogs would often dig up and feed on the dead bodies. Canis is the Latin word for dog.
The Etruscans named this hill VATICANUS, meaning *habitation of dogs.*
Consider the word CARNIVAL:
Later, a Roman ruler named Caligula drained this site, and held enormously popular carnivals (carnival is Latin for *flesh-raising*).
The word **mazzaroth** refers to the lights of the heavens collectively, not the belief there are signs written in the skies using **zoo** animals adapted from Nimrod's Astro-Babel. See more at this webpage:
fossilizedcustoms.com/zodiac.html

Redemption Without Repentance?
Reading Romans chapters 6 through 8 opens-up the Truth of what Paul was really saying. Lacking the Spirit of Yahusha, a person *cannot* obey, nor *wants* to obey. An unrepentant person only obeys their will.
Is the Turah sin? Shall we continue in sin to let favor increase? Pastors struggle to understand Paul's writings. The understanding of the Turah (instruction) is given to us by the indwelling of Yahusha, and Paul shows the difference between the mind of the *flesh*, and the mind of the *Spirit*:
"I find therefore this law, that when I wish to do the good, that the evil is present with me. For I

delight in the Turah of Yahuah according to the inward man, but I see another law in my body, battling against the Turah of my mind, and bringing me into captivity to the law of sin which is in my body." Romans 7:21-23 BYNV

Paul says he delights in the Turah of Yahuah, but the mind of the flesh battles with the mind of the Spirit within him (inner man). He acknowledges Yahusha rescues him from acting on the evil his flesh would otherwise overtake him in. The letter to the Galatians is regarding circumcising the flesh of adult males (decided against at Acts 15 for new converts). Yahusha writes a love for His Commandments on our hearts, and we walk in them. The mind of the flesh cannot obey, nor does it desire to obey.

What we have inherited from our fathers is *futility*, not *careful instruction*.
Which do you prefer, futility or careful instruction?
There is only one Name given by which we must be delivered (Acts 4:12).

THIRD COMMANDMENT OF THE DECALOGUE
The Decalogue, *The Ten Words*, in Hebrew is:
ASERETH HA DABARIM
The Ten Commandments / Words are vows we pledge from our heart to obey our Husband YAHUAH, and thereby we become His wife.
The Covenant is eternal, and is a marriage Yahuah's bride is committed to. The mixed-multitude Yahuah delivered from Egypt became one nation by going through water, then joined to Yahuah's eternal Covenant at Sinai (Ex 20:1-17). His Covenant of marriage will never pass away.

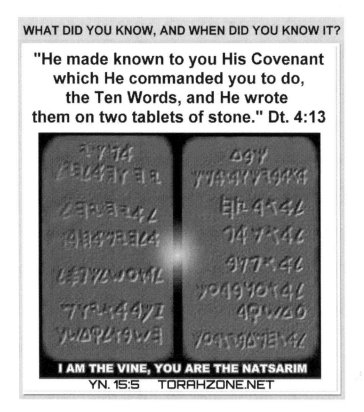

WHAT DID YOU KNOW, AND WHEN DID YOU KNOW IT?

"He made known to you His Covenant
which He commanded you to do,
the Ten Words, and He wrote
them on two tablets of stone." Dt. 4:13

I AM THE VINE, YOU ARE THE NATSARIM
YN. 15:5   TORAHZONE.NET

In the *Preface* of most English versions of Scripture, the translators admit replacing the Name of YAHUAH with a *device* because of men's traditions, so we see "*LORD*" where the Name of YAHUAH should appear. This word was translated in the Anglican Catholic KJV from the Latin Vulgate word *DOMINUS* (lord), translated from the Greek *KYRIOS* (lord), translated from the Hebrew *ADUNI* (lord). The true Name, YAHUAH (four vowels *yod-hay-uau-hay*) has been deleted, yet it is used far more than any other word in Scripture.

The Hebrew word *closest in meaning* to LORD is *BEL*. LORD, used as a proper name to substitute for YAHUAH's Name, is *way, way beyond **blasphemy**. BAAL* is not the living Alahim; this was decided at Mt. Karmel by AliYahu (1 Kings 18).

YAHUSHA, Or JESUS; NOT BOTH

Equivocating teachers never penetrate to the foundation: Hebrew. YAHUSHA is an actual word you can find 216 times (**yod-hay-uau-shin-ayin**) in the **TaNaK** (see an interlinear at Zek. 3). Slowly enunciate the sound of each letter in the Hebrew spelling: **yod-hay-uau-shin-ayin**.

It's a word based on **Yahuah**, with a simple suffix, *shin-ayin* (SHA). It's the same suffix we see in the name "ALISHA" (vowel distortions introduced in the 8th century caused this name to be transliterated *ELISHA*).

The **"only Name given among men by which we must be delivered"** (Acts 4:12) is <u>Hebrew</u>, so if we are seeking the foundation, skip the Latin and Greek, and go to the source. Those who dig for it will find the Truth, and never go back to compromise with alterations, opinions of habit, or fear of losing credibility. Yahusha's Name has been ravaged, and we are seeing His Name "turning the world upside-down" again.

From His perspective, *the world is turning right-side up again.*

IESV: KJV Based On Latin Vulgate
How they Taught The World To Say *"JESUS"*

The Anglican Catholic KJV is basically the Latin Vulgate brought over into English, completed in 1611. Gutenburg had printed dozens of copies of the Latin Vulgate during the 1450's. The errors in it and the KJV are identical, except for the term "Easter," which the Anglican Catholic KJV inserted at Acts 12:4 in place of the Latin word for Pesak, Pascha. The Latin Vulgate reads <u>IESV</u> or IESVS (in place of the true Name, Yahusha), and the first edition of the KJV also used IESV. The V – shape is sounded U. In subsequent decades after dozens of revisions and the new letter "J," the KJV changed the IESV to Jesu, and finally Jesus in the 1800's.

How Did The Christian Theologians Not Understand Mt. 26:17?

Both the Latin Vulgate and the KJV make it seem the Yahusha's Natsarim (disciples) had asked Him where He wished them to prepare the Passover *"On the first day of Matsah."* That would be impossible; He was lying in the borrowed tomb on the first day of Matsah, and no one could talk to Him; Passover was already over!

Often the term "Passover" can refer to the whole period from the 14th through the seven days of Matsah, but Matsah is quite specific. This is especially so when it is expressed as "on the first day of Matsah."

Many other translators followed the Latin Vulgate, and did not properly understand the appointed times. They defend their errors in the footnotes with all manner of special explanations, but the Truth is always best, and simple (equivocating is a Jesuit tactic).

The Latin Vulgate at Mt. 26:17 reads this way:

"Prima autem die azymorum accesserunt discipuli ad Iesum, dicentes: Ubi vis paremus tibi comedere Pascha?"

Gutenburg eBook for the passage at Matthew 26:17, which modern translators altered for contemporary consumers (IESV was changed to Jesus for modern readers):

"And on the first day of the Azymes, the disciples came to Jesus, saying: Where wilt thou that we prepare for thee to eat the pasch?"

65

Foreign *translators* have made this same unique mistake, and what are called *Hebrew-based English translations* must have been reverse-translations into Aramaic script based on one of the many copies of the Latin Vulgate produced by Gutenburg in Mainz, Germany spread into the world during the 1450's. The Christian translators dismiss the importance of the appointed times, so when shown these mistakes they seem to not care to acknowledge them as serious. Some of us care a great deal, and making it seem that the appointed times don't matter much helps explain why Christianity never observed any of them. They have no Passover, but claim to know the Passover Lamb.

STRONG'S CONCORDANCE - 1890

James Strong published an exhaustive concordance based on the KJV in 1890, and except for the influences of the niqqud markings of the Masoretes (8th-century vowel directions), and using letters non-existent in the Eberith script, his efforts helped many people penetrate deeper into the definitions of words, and the context they are used in.

The Anglican Catholic *KJV* was greatly influenced by the niqqud marks of the Masoretes (8th century vowel additions), and James Strong went along with them.

The BYNV is different from any other translation you'll find, and corrects the meaning of words, phrases, and references concerning the festivals of Yahuah that traditional Christian translators missed due to being unfamiliar with the way Yahusha lived.

THIRD COMMANDMENT:

"You do not cast ... (Hebrew, *NASA*, meaning lift up, send, throw) ... *the Name of YAHUAH your Alahim to ruin* . . . (Hebrew, *SHOAH*, meaning *devastation*) ... *for YAHUAH your Alahim will not hold anyone guiltless who casts His Name to ruin."*

Read the Preface of most English translations, and they will admit they threw the Name of Yahuah out, claiming it's "tradition," and used a device in place of it: *LORD*.

Why violate the Name of YAHUAH by hiding, changing, or replacing it with another term equivalent to the meaning of BEL? BEL is the Kanaanite storm deity worshiped by the priests supported by Iezebel. She was the witch-wife of Ahab, and her name means *devoted to BEL*. She was a Sidonian princess, and supported the priests of BEL and ASHERAH. She was eaten by dogs.

All of Ahab's male descendants were cut-off because he allowed BEL to be worshiped rather than Yahuah (1 Kings 21:21, 2 Kings 9:8).

From Yahuah's perspective, have you been programmed to worship BEL (*LORD*) without being conscious of it?

YAHUSHA (Hebrew, *yod-hay-uau-shin-ayin*): The Name above all names was first used by Mushah for Husha at Numbers 13:16. HUSHA (*hay-uau-shin-ayin*) means *deliverer*, and YAHUSHA means *I am your Deliverer*.

Notice how YAHUAH's Name shares the same first three letters (*yod-hay-uau*), YAHU. The conquerors of the people, Nicolaitanes (Revelation 2:6-15) were, and still are, *doctrinal overlords* who deceptively explain everything to the gullible masses who place their trust in them. Their explanation of the word JESUS does not begin with the original Hebrew Name Yahusha, because it would never produce the sound they struggle to explain.

The Nicolaitanes' explanation uses the Greek language, which does not have the alphabetical letters necessary to transliterate the sound of the real Name. Notice how JESUS sounds like IE-ZUS, hailing the Greek deity Zeus. The Greek letters IESOUS (IHSOYS prior to the lower-case letter forms) was an intentional substitution to conceal the Name.

Transliterating into the Latin, an encrypted christogram **IC-XC** was used in the eastern empire. The christogram **IHS** was used in the west. The Latin Vulgate translation (391-403) used the christogram **IESV**. It was the first major printing endeavor of Johannes Gutenberg's movable type press in 1455. This Catholic translation was used to produce the Anglican Catholic KJV. The IESV is preserved in the earliest editions, but the revised edition of 1885 is what the world now uses, believing that JESUS is correct. *He-soos* in the Hebrew language means *the horse*; in Latin it means *the pig*. Arabs use the word **ISA**, which sounds closest to *ESU* (*ayin-shin-uau*), aka Esau (a word meaning *hairy*). After all, Yahuah told us, "I am YAHUAH; that is My Name." (YashaYahu 42:8)

Notice another huge blunder tradition has given to us:

GOD *[god]* as defined by the 1945 *Encyclopedia Americana:*
"Common Teutonic word for personal object of religious worship, formerly applicable to super-

human beings of heathen myth; on conversion of Teutonic races to Christianity, term was applied to Supreme Being."

Turning aside to myths happens. *What could possibly go wrong? (see Malaki. 4, 2 Timothy 4)*

WHAT IS HIS NAME?

Please consider these words carefully: Yahuah is not *the LORD* (BEL). Every false translation admits in its preface they have rejected the key of knowledge. The Stone (Ps. 118:26) the builders have rejected is the Name of Yahuah (yod-hay-uau-hay, 4 vowels), and their own prefaces admit they used a device, LORD, brought to them through traditions from former false translations that used Dominus, Kyrios, Aduni, and all refer to the Eberith word BEL (beth-ayin-lamed). Mt. Karmel's lesson still needs to be proclaimed so all mankind will call on the Name that AliYahu called on which brought the fire from Yahuah upon the offering. Our tongues are the altar from which we offer true praise and thanksgiving to Yahuah. "I am Yahuah; that is My Name . . . " (YashaYahu 42:8)

The Revelation Of The Identity Of Yahusha: ALEF-TAU

If we don't know we're confused, someone needs to be sent to tell us. We were misled from childhood. Some try to make us accept what they teach with men's ideas, saying *name doesn't mean name,* or *He has many names,* or *He came in the authority.* They want to be teachers of the Word, but never able to come to an understanding of the Truth. (2 Tim. 3:7)

"Who has gone up to the shamayim and come down?
Who has gathered the wind in His fists?
Who has bound the mayim in a garment?
Who established all the ends of the arets?
What is His Name, and what is His Son's Name,
If you know it? Every Word of Aluah is tried; He is
a shield to those taking refuge in Him. Do not add
to His Words, lest He reprove you, and you be
found a liar." Proverbs 30:4-6

Yahukanon 5:43: *"I have come in My Father's Name and you do not receive Me; if another comes in his own name, him you would receive."*
We are hated because we belong to Yahusha, the Vine, and we are the Natsarim. If they hated Him, they will hate us also.

We are hated for Yahusha's Name even today. Anti-missionaries post their opposition to the true Name all over the Internet, and spread gossip to malign those who use it.
Shaul <u>was</u> an anti-missionary, but Yahusha showed him how much <u>he</u> would *suffer for His Name.*
Paul (the name we know him by today) was a hunter of the Natsarim, but then became the hunted after his conversion, and was accused of being a ringleader of the Natsarim after he abandoned the false *"traditions of the fathers."* People argue that the Name should not be uttered, or that Yahuah will hear us even if we deny His Name and use other names because *"the people would not know who we are referring to."*
My point exactly – and whose fault is that? By teaching error, they are no closer to the Truth at all. Our teachers have not taught us, and so the guyim (nations) will come from the ends of the Earth in the

last days and say, *"Our fathers have inherited nothing but futility and lies."*
Even the confused languages can still call on His Name, and may record it in their foreign scripts. The translators admit altering it for tradition, replacing the four letters of the Hebrew with LORD. Read any the prefaces and all will tell you how they handle the Name. Names are not translated, they are transliterated. Look at what happened at 1 Kings 18 on Mt. Karmel with the priests of the LORD (BEL). Psalm 102:18 tells us His Name is written so people to be created may call (utter, say) His Name. YashaYahu (Isaiah) 42:8 says "I am Yahuah, that is My Name . . . " and goes on to explain further. Mal. 3 says Yahuah listened to those who think upon His Name, and called them His *treasured possession.*

Yahusha - Prove It For Yourself
Look up Zechariah 3 in an Interlinear Hebrew-English version.
The Eberith language spells the name of the Kohen ha Gadol with 5 letters. This spelling is shown in the TaNaK 216 times (yod-hay-uau-shin-ayin). Look at Numbers 13:16 for the first use of this name.
Mushah added 1 letter to **Husha** (son of Nun):
yod + hay-uau-shin-ayin.
The *script* shown in most Interlinear Scriptures is Aramith (inherited from the time of the 70-year captivity), a transliteration of the Eberith language. We are attempting to use Latin script right now to phonetically duplicate the sounds of Eberith words. Widely-accepted alterations came along in the 8th century disguised as speech guides known as niqqud marks.

Question: In reality, is the suffix SHA in the name ALISHA written any differently than the same suffix in the name YAHUSHA?

A collective false memory is at work in populations, and the first 3 letters (yod-hay-uau) are intentionally programmed out by mind-controlling grammar rules. There are no niqqud marks in any of the scrolls found at Qumran because such added marks were invented in the 8th century by Karaites living at Babel.

The language (and script) we understand as "Hebrew" is not Aramaic, Egyptian, or Akkadian, but it has been mislabeled as a Greek word, Phoenician. It is what we should refer to as Eberith, the same script Danial read on the wall (Dan. 5). At YashaYahu (Isaiah) 36:11 you will see the words "EBERITH" and "ARAMITH" in the original text, and then you will understand better. We are not unable to learn, our teachers have confused us with what they accepted, and we need to unlearn and reread so we can be set free by the Truth.

The Nimrod Effect is older and more comprehensive than the Mandela Effect, but you'll never see it until Yahusha opens your eyes to it.

The **first** and **last** letters of the Hebrew **Alef-Beth** are mysteriously placed near the Covenant Name (identity) of **Yahuah** throughout the Scriptures. It is an identity marker of the First and the Last, finally revealed by Yahusha ha Mashiak as **Himself** at Rev. 1:8.

The beast apparatus is the *world order* filled with deception for those who reject receiving a love for the Truth. For most of the past 2000 years, the influence of eastern *mysticism* and *Gnostic enlightenment* has dominated the western world.

This **Gnosticism** has multiplied itself and is now seen *everywhere*, posing as the various forms of religion, all posturing themselves to be the only truth. At the core of them all is the worship of the *host of heaven* (Zodiac/Astrology), originating in Babel's worship of *Nimrod, Semiramis, and Tammuz.* This is the premise of Alexander Hislop's book **The Two Babylons**.

The false worship of the Sun, Moon, planets, and constellations (Zodiac, zoo animals, *host of heaven*) manifests itself in the haloes, **three heads**, and sometimes **triple pairs of arms** depicted in statues.

Beads, flowers, *nimbuses* (haloes), ashes, and meditation positions are just a few of the aspects of Babel's false worship. The majority of the circus fathers were originally followers of **Manichaeism**, a religion founded by **Mani** (216-277CE).

Manichaeism was a major **Gnostic religion**, originating in Sassanid-era Babylonia.

Mani's Gnostic teachings about Yahusha became the pattern seen in many tenets of Christianity, adopted through the *church fathers*. These pretenders are often referred to as *men of the cloth.* wearing their special robes as we see with any other uniformed professional.

The people of Beroia (Acts 17) checked Scripture to **validate** *everything* they heard. Since that time, **Gnostic beliefs** were adopted, and it was taught that the Creator is THREE, not ONE as the **Shema** states. This has been promoted so well that *any who challenge that premise are regarded as heretics.* For a moment, let's think **outside that box** (prison, stronghold), and go with the working premise that the Creator is **ONE**, as He claims He is.

What If Someone Asked You . . . to <u>test</u> all things you hear from other human beings? The Word of Yahuah is maligned all day long, and His Name is blasphemed continually. Yahuah is Yahusha; there is no other before, or coming after Him. The world is trained to disobey, and to call on a false name as their deliverer.

Google YAHUSHA, and you will discern the wrath of those who resist the only Name given among mankind by which we must be delivered (Acts 4:12).

Yahuah is One; He has become our Deliverer. YAHUSHA means *"I am your Deliverer."* The name JESUS is less than 500 years old.

What does the name JESUS mean? They may argue it means IESV, ISA, IESOUS, JEZUS, IHS and others.

The **Stone** the builders ***rejected*** is the key of knowledge, and their replacement of the true Name is admitted in the Prefaces of their translations. Are you willing to do the work and test everything, or remain like the simple, those who believe every word they hear? The clever one watches his steps (Prov. 14:15).

Yahusha declared that He and the Father are **one**: let's hypothetically take that statement as being literal. If Yahuah entered into His physical world and ***appeared*** as one of us, that which we could see and touch of Him would be His "son" revealing Himself just as the opening words of Hebrews explain:

Heb 1:1-6: **"Alahim, having of old spoken in many portions and many ways to the fathers by the prophets, has in these last days spoken to us** (by or as) **the Son, whom He has appointed heir of**

74

all, through whom also He made the ages, Who being the brightness of the esteem and the <u>exact</u> representation of His substance, and sustaining all by the Word of His power, having made a cleansing of our sins through Himself, sat down at the right hand of the Greatness on high, having become so much better than the messengers, as He has inherited a more excellent Name than them. For to which of the messengers did He ever say, 'You are My Son, today I have brought You forth?' And again, 'I shall be to Him a Father, and He shall be to Me a Son?' And when He again brings the first-born into the world, He says, 'Let all the messengers of Alahim do reverence to Him.'"

Yahusha's enemies understood **exactly** what He was saying, and they stated their understanding in the context of Yahusha's declaration that He is *one and the same* as the Father:

John / Yahukanon 10:30-33:
"'I and My Father are one.' Again the Yahudim picked up stones to stone Him. Yahusha answered them, 'Many good works I have shown you from My Father. Because of which of these works do you stone Me?'
The Yahudim answered Him, saying, 'We do not stone You for a good work, but for blasphemy, and because You, being a <u>Man</u>, make Yourself <u>Alahim</u>.'" *they definitely knew what He meant!*

Yn. 14:6-10: "**Yahusha said to him, 'I am the Way, and the Truth, and the Life. No one comes to the Father except through Me.**
If you had known Me, you would have known My Father too. From now on you know Him, and have

seen.'

Philip said to Him, "Master, show us the Father, and it is enough for us." Yahusha said to him,

'Have I been with you so long, and you have not known Me, Philip? He who has seen <u>Me</u> has seen the <u>Father</u>, and how do you say,

'Show us the Father'? Do you not believe that I am in the Father, and the Father is in Me? The words that I speak to you I do not speak from Myself.

But the Father who stays in Me does His works.'"

AL SHADDAI HAS BLOOD?

The Hebrew Eberith term **Al Shaddai** means mighty-one almighty. It's the idea of Yahuah being *overwhelmingly lofty*; He is literally *most high*.

The term **Al** indicates mighty or lofty-one. He's unrestrainable, powerful, and way, *way* beyond our comprehension. It's used in the name of the Israeli airline, **EL-AL**, meaning *"to go upward"* (ayin-lamed, alef-lamed, EL-AL).

The term "**shaddai**" indicates all-sufficiency.

Acts 20:28 says the Ruach haQodesh purchased us with **His own blood**. The Spirit of Alahim has shed His own blood. He is the Helper, the Paraklita, and dwells in us.

The **identity** of Al Shaddai is revealed in two places:

Exo 6:2,3: **"And Alahim spoke to Mosheh and said to him, 'I am Yahuah.**

And I appeared to Abraham, to Yitshaq, and to Yaqub, as Al Shaddai. And by My Name, Yahuah, was I not known to them?"

Rev 1:8: **"'I am the Alef and the Tau, Beginning and End,' says Yahuah, 'Who is and Who was and Who is to come, the Almighty.'"**

The "Almighty" (Shaddai) is revealed to be Yahusha,

as well as the **literal meaning** of "Yahuah" in the statement, "Who **is** and Who **was** and Who *is to come."*

A Name Is Personal

I am that I am is often heard in sermons around the world, but it lacks sense in English. The Eberith is: AHAYAH ASHER AHAYAH.

The Eberith / Hebrew meaning of the phrase is, *"I will be Who I will be."* Another deceptive teaching insists that Yahuah Name is AMANUAL.

These deceptions prey on the innocent, knowing the masses are too easily taken-in with false impressions. AMANUAL is Yahuah's *renown,* or what He is *KNOWN* for, and it's a title, but not a personal name.

Yahuah is His Name forever, and His memorial to all generations (Ex. 3:15).

Yahuah declares this at YashaYahu / Is. 42:8:

"I am Yahuah; that is My Name." (read the whole context, and you will get the sense that it's very, very clear how He feels about His Name.

fossilizedcustoms.com/name.html

WHO IS YAHUSHA?

Yahusha's identity has been debated in countless disputes, and His identity cannot be known *unless it is revealed to you by Him:*

Luke 10:22-24: "'**All has been delivered to Me by My Father, and no one knows Who the Son is, except the Father, and Who the Father is, except the Son, and he to whom the Son wishes to reveal Him.'**

And turning to His taught ones He said, separately, 'Blessed are the eyes that see what you see, for I say to you that many prophets and sovereigns

have wished to see what you see, and have not seen it, and to hear what you hear, and have not heard it.'"

Who the Son is, and Who the Father is, is **unknown** except to *"he to whom the Son wishes to reveal."* The greatest declaration of all, affirmed by Yahusha, is the Shema (Dt. 6:4), that Yahuah is <u>one</u>.
Who is the Mashiak? Is there any deliverer or Redeemer, other than Yahuah? He says no.

Isa / YashaYahu49:26:
"'And I will feed them that oppress you with their own flesh; and they shall be drunken with their own blood, as with sweet wine: and all flesh shall know that I Yahuah *am* your Saviour and your Redeemer, the Mighty One of Yaqub.'"

YashaYahu / Isaiah 44:24:
Thus said Yahuah, your Redeemer, and He who formed you from the womb, 'I am Yahuah, doing all, stretching out the heavens *all alone*, spreading out the Earth, with *none beside Me . . .*'"

Emmanuel, Prince of Peace, Everlasting Father, Mighty Alahim all refer to ONE Being.
At Revelation chapter 1 quoted above, we find the One speaking calling Himself the Almighty (Shaddai). He further states He is the "***living One; and I was dead, and behold, I am alive forevermore.***"
Micah, the prophet, at 5:2 tells us that Bethlehem Ephrathah would have One "***go forth for Me to be Ruler in Yisharal. His goings forth are from long ago, from the days of eternity***."
There is only <u>**one**</u> eternal Being, and He tells us there is no one beside Him, and identifies Himself as *the* ***first and the last*** (YashaYahu 41:4, 44:6).

"I, I am Yahuah, and besides Me there is no Deliverer." - YashaYahu 43:11

"Fear not, neither be afraid: have I not declared to you of old, and showed it? and you are my witnesses. Is there any Alahim besides me? yea, there is no Rock; I know not any." YashaYahu44:8

Yahusha is **the Stone** the builders rejected.
There aren't *TWO* Rocks.

When Yahusha told Yahukanon to record the Words to the assemblies, He called Himself *Al Shaddai.* In the same sentence, He provided the answer to the mystery of the ages: Who the *Alef-Tau* is. Ultimately, the **Father** reconciled the world's sin debt by taking that debt on to Himself by His Fullness dwelling in His Son, and shedding **His Blood** for our redemption.

He is alive forevermore, the First-fruits of all Creation. The Father ultimately receives the honor; He is reconciling us.

"Alahim, therefore, has highly exalted Him and given Him the Name which is above every name, that at the Name of Yahusha every knee should bow, of those in heaven, and of those on Earth, and of those under the earth, and every tongue should confess that Yahuah is Yahusha ha Mashiak, to the esteem of Alahim the Father." Phil. 2:9-11

ALL SCRIPTURE BEARS WITNESS OF YAHUSHA
"You search the Scriptures, because you think you possess everlasting life in them. And these are the ones that bear witness of Me." - Yn 5:39

YAHUSHA: *"I AM YOUR DELIVERER"*
"I have come in My Father's Name and you do not receive Me, if another comes in his own name, him you would receive." - Yn. 5:43

Yahuah is **the Rock** of Ages.

Yahuah Himself is the Mashiak, the Melek (King) of Yisharal. *All Scripture brings us to this essential conclusion.*

He is acting in the role of a SON, and as an actor might take up a **persona** (mask). Yahuah took the <u>form</u> of a servant, and came to be in the <u>likeness</u> of men. Trinitarians call this view or oneness *modalism.*
We call on <u>Yahuah</u> as our *Deliverer* in the Name we are to be immersed in: **YAHUSHA**
This uniquely means *"I am your Deliverer."*

WHAT IS HIS NAME, IF YOU KNOW IT?
"For I am more stupid than anyone, and do not have the understanding of a man. And I have not learned wisdom that I should know the knowledge of the Set-apart One. Who has gone up to the heavens and come down? Who has gathered the wind in His fists? Who has bound the waters in a garment? Who established all the ends of the Earth? What is His Name, And what is His Son's Name, If you know it?" - Pro 30:2-4

The revelation of Yahusha's true identity is revealed by what we just read, And what He said about Himself in His human form:
"And no one has gone up into the heaven except He Who came down from the heaven – the Son of Adam." – Yn. 3:13

"Who, being in the form of Alahim, did not regard equality with Alahim a matter to be grasped, but emptied Himself, taking the <u>form</u> of a servant, and came to be in the <u>likeness</u> of men.
And having been found in <u>fashion</u> as a man, He

humbled Himself and became obedient unto death, death even of a stake." -Php. 2:6-8

Yahusha is the **Right Hand** of Yahuah. He is the **power**, the mighty Right Hand. In the "**Day of Distress,**" the nations will realize Who Yahusha is:

YirmeYahu 16:19-21:
"O Yahuah, my strength and my stronghold and my refuge, in the day of distress the gentiles shall come to You from the ends of the Earth and say, 'Our fathers have inherited only falsehood, futility, and there is no value in them.' Would a man make mighty ones for himself, which are not mighty ones? Therefore see, I am causing them to know, this time I cause them to know My hand and My might.
And they shall know that My Name is Yahuah!"

A name reveals the personal, unique IDENTITY of a person or thing it is assigned to. Even the word **noun** refers to the name of something.
The *Alef-Tau* reveals the identity of Who is speaking throughout Scripture.
That day has come; we know His Name has been hidden, and we understand Who He is.
"'And now, what have I here,' declares Yahuah, 'that My people are taken away for naught? Those who rule over them make them wail,' declares Yahuah, 'and My Name is despised all day continually. Therefore My people shall know My Name, in that day, for I am the One who is speaking. See, it is I.'"
YashaYahu 52:5-6; See also YashaYahu 42:8

Those who rule over His people had been making them *wail* or *howl* because they were not speaking

His Name, being deceived to call on *BEL* (aka BAAL).

BARUK HABA BASHEM YAHUAH
"Blessed is He who is coming in the Name of Yahuah! We shall bless you from the House of Yahuah." - Psa 118:26

Now we understand the meaning of Yahusha's Words when He said:
"See, your House is left to you laid waste. And truly I say to you, you shall by no means see Me until *the time* comes when you say, 'Blessed is He who is coming in the Name of Yahuah!"
Luke 13:35; See also Revelation 14:1

Yahuah is Yahusha
Translators have hidden the true Name of our Creator Yahuah by replacing it with the Hebrew word ADUNI / **adonai** (my lord), then the Greek **kurios** (lord), then the Latin **dominus** (lord), and then the Anglican Catholic KJV used the Latin Vulgate to render dominus in English, producing **LORD**.
This is not His Name.

He is ALEF-TAU, THE BEGINNING AND END
Who can forgive sins? Only *the one who has been offended* can forgive an offense.

Worshiping A Deity Called *LORD?*

YESHUA or YAHUSHA?

The difference in transliteration between YAHUSHA and YAHUSHUA is obviously the second letter U. In Scripture, we find the name of the man the world knows as "JOSHUA" spelled with 5 letters (YOD-HAY-UAU-SHIN-AYIN) 216 times, and with six letters (YOD-HAY-UAU-SHIN-UAU-AYIN) 2 times. The modifier, or suffix, is the ending part of either transliteration (SHA, or SHUA). This suffix means "deliverer," based on the root, YASHA (YOD-SHIN-AYIN). SHA is the sound of this suffix, and express in the transliteration ALISHA (aka Elisha). This man's name means *"my Alahim is deliverer."* Also, the root YASHA (YOD-SHIN-AYIN) is seen in another prophet's name: YASHAYAHU (aka **Isa-iah**).

Why are there differences? Shortening a name is common today, and not a new idea.

The most-used form is YAHUSHA, and uses five Hebrew letters. At Numbers 13:16 we see the name of the son of Nun spelled with four letters, YOD-SHIN-UAU-AYIN (a common word for "helper" or "deliver" yet lacking the Name of Yahuah as a part of it. This is only used *once* as a proper noun (name). We should teach the form that is found in overwhelming numbers in Scripture: YOD-HAY-UAU-SHIN-AYIN; "YAHUSHA."

What is His Name, and what is His Son's Name, if you know it?

For more, visit: **fossilizedcustoms.com/name.html**

Be Careful How You Hear

"For I am more stupid than anyone, and do not have the understanding of a man. And I have not learned wisdom That I should know the knowledge of the Qodesh One. Who has gone up to the shamayim and come down? Who has gathered the wind in His fists? Who has bound the mayim in a garment? Who established all the ends of the arets? What is His Name, And what is His Son's Name, If you know it? Every Word of Aluah is tried; He is a shield to those taking refuge in Him. Do not add to His Words, lest He reprove you, and you be found a liar. Two things I have asked of You –

Deny them not to me before I die: Remove falsehood and a lying word far from me; give me neither poverty nor riches; Feed me my portion of bread; lest I become satisfied and deny You, and say, "Who is Yahuah?"

Proverbs 30:2-9

There is only one Name we must call on for deliverance (Acts 4:12, YashaYahu 42:8). His Name is His seal. Remember Mt. Karmel?

Our *moral foundation* does not rest on any religion fabricated by men.

It rests on the personal relationship with our Creator, Yahuah, Who revealed His will to all mankind - those present, and not present - at Sinai. The Ten Commandments are the eternal Covenant, and animal blood (the old covenant) was placed beside the ark (Dt. 31:26, Hebrews 8:13). Yahusha offered His blood that ended the old covenant requiring animal blood. For those trusting in His perfect offering of Himself, He causes us to love His eternal Covenant, by circumcising our hearts with a love for obedience. All the lies of the dragon are dispelled when the Truth is accepted, so please let Yahusha throw out the old leaven, and allow us to enter into the coming reign without men's guile. Who's with us? We are Natsarim - Google us, and spread the message to guard The Ten Commandments, the message of AliYahu (Malaki 4).

Distress Of Nations

The Temple Mount is the Nexus Point for the World. The destruction of the Temple in 70 CE began the distress. Yahusha wept over Jerusalem because they did not recognize the time of their visitation.
The world will not recognize their time either.
Danial spoke of an abomination we would recognize in time, and many would receive understanding, then a great distress would engulf the whole world.
The catalyst is perceiving what is on the Temple Mount, standing in the place it should not be.
We are the watchmen, the Natsarim Search Team, ambassadors of the reign of Yahusha. We are waiting for Him, and we guard His Commandments.

THEY DON'T KNOW WHAT THEY DON'T KNOW

Without expecting it, many will hear *"I never knew you,"* and be astounded.

The lawless don't know what they don't know.

They are not in any covenant with Yahusha, although it is always open to them to accept. They are trained to believe obedience is unnecessary; the very idea is bitter to them.

Psalm 50:16 says,

"But to the lawless Alahim said, 'What right have you to recite My laws, Or take My Covenant in your mouth, While you hated instruction and cast My Words behind you?'"

The *traditions of the fathers* was Paul's former way of life, and will pass away. Yahusha's Words will never pass away, and He lived a perfect walk of obedience in His Word to show us what perfection is. The Ten Commandments are the walk, yet men teach against walking in them. Malaki 4:1-6 tells us to guard them, or Yahuah will destroy the entire Earth.

OUR ACTIONS SHOW OUR BELIEF, OR OUR BELIEF IS DEAD
Just Believe? Even Demons Believe

We've inherited lies from our fathers.

If we continue in sin, we don't know Yahusha.

If we are not in the eternal Covenant, we may believe just as much as the demons do, but without understanding what sin is, repenting, and trusting in Yahusha's blood for our complete redemption, just belief without actions means our belief is dead. He enters our mind, sharing His perspective, and gives us His help. This is why Yahusha is called Helper (Paraklita). The old covenant is obsolete (animal blood, former priesthood). Read Dt. 31:26, then Hebrews 8:13, and Yahusha will help you see the Truth even through the bad translations. Ask Him if

you can continue to ignore and break the Commandments, and He'll tell you.
He tells us the answer at 1 Yahukanon / Jn. 2:4.

DAY OF YAHUAH

The Day Of Yahuah Is Coming Like An Oven
There's useful research on the end of days from Scripture in my books REAPERS and RETURN OF YAHUSHA. Birth pangs are going on big-time even now. It's only my opinion, but the pressure / distress has been going on since the destruction of the Temple (70 CE) by Titus and Vespasian. Emblematic of this is the celebrated Arch of Titus at Rome. This arch displays the carved relief of soldiers taking away the golden menorah.
Also, consider what is standing on the Temple Mount right now. They don't yet **observe** it, but when it is recognized as the abomination built ***"in the place it should not be,"*** the **distress** will become very fierce. Those in the land prematurely will be eaten by birds (*excarnation;* Ez. 39, Jer. 7, Is. 56, Rev. 19). Yahusha will pour out His burning wrath on all

disobedient mankind. We know it will be in a 7th month, but only Yahuah knows the exact time.
fossilizedcustoms.com/mark.html

Don't Wait For The Asteroids

The plagues have begun; don't wait for the asteroids. One of the things you may have noticed about the Natsarim is how different our perspective of Yahuah's Word is from the World Order around us.

The names of the days of the week, the idolatrous fertility festivals camouflaging their original meanings, and the trust most people place in the World Order will never survive the Second Coming of Yahusha. He told us to look at the fruit to identify the tree.

He said *"I am the Vine; you are the Natsarim."*

If they hated Him, they will hate His followers also. YirmeYahu 16:19, Mt. 24, YashaYahu 24, and Danial 12 all describe the end of days, and the same period of great distress. Don't wait for the asteroids.
fossilizedcustoms.com/before.html

Los Lunas Stone

An Ancient Gate-Stone in New Mexico, USA

The tilted shape of the letter yod demonstrates this Decalogue stone was inscribed by someone

influenced by Eberith from very ancient times. Covered for millennia with vines and lichen, it was originally a gate stone. The order to write the Decalogue on your doorposts and gates is found at Dt. 6:9. Due to the extreme age of the inscription, it was most likely before the tax revolt that split the tribes, so Shalomoh was most likely still reigning over all the tribes. Yisharal's ports and ship building materials were mostly in the northward area, and the large area above Yahudah was Afraim's domain. Shalomoh had dealings with the king of Tyre, which helped build and sail on the huge ships. Tyre and Sidon were harbors where a huge amount of trading went on. The *way of the sea* brought the Torah to the ends of the Earth. Zebulon was mentioned in Yaqub's blessing on his 12 sons this way: *"Zebulun shall dwell by the seashore and become a harbor for ships; his border shall extend to Sidon."*
Barashith / Gen. 49:13

The Los Lunas Stone Tapestry
The letters / script of Eberith appear nothing like the Aramith script brought back from Babel with Ezra & NekemYah after the 70-year captivity. Their script *transliterated* the Eberith language, and could be read aloud without the niqqud marks invented almost 1200 years later. Danial had to be called to read the Eberith writing on the wall for the babblers at Babel. The dots and dashes invented in the 8th century CE are truly what is fake, yet endorsed by all the scholars. ALEF is A; BETH is B; GIMEL is G; and other letters written in real Eberith script convey the sounds of the letters in order to pronounce the words. Phonology has endured great pressure from outside languages due to the expulsions, but also from the influences of the rules most Yahudim are

taught. The Los Lunas Stone shows the Ten Commandments from the period of King Shalomoh (Solomon), and is another example of the appearance of the Name seen on the great scroll seen in the Hekal Sefer (Shrine of the Book) in Jerusalem, Israel today. That scroll, and the stone at Los Lunas, both show a more authentic script than most people are taught with. The first to state his case seems right, until another cross-examines him.

CONSPIRACY!

THE SCROLL OF YASHAYAHU

PLACED AMONG THE DEAD SEA SCROLLS APPROXIMATELY 125 BCE
IT HAS NO NIQQUD MARKS, PHONEMES, OR SPEECH GUIDES

YOD-HAY-UAU-HAY

"YAHUAH"

The Great Isaiah Scroll

TORAH INSTITUTE RESEARCH

THE JARS PRESERVED THE NAME FOR US TODAY, AS ANY DOCUMENT HAVING THE NAME ON IT
WAS CAREFULLY HANDLED WITH GREAT RESPECT, NEVER TREATED PROFANELY

WINDOW   HOOK   WINDOW   HAND

Hebrew is the source of our letter A:

TORAH INSTITUTE   TORAHZONE.NET

NEWS FLASH!
ALEF IS AN "A"

HUH?

ADAM
ADAM MEANS RED GROUND

ARETS
ARETS IS HEBREW FOR EARTH, SOIL, OR LAND

ALAHIM
ALAHIM MEANS ELEVATED, HIGH, UPWARD, MIGHTY ONE

ABRAHIM
ABRAHIM MEANS FATHER OF NATIONS, MULTITUDES

AND IT'S A VOWEL

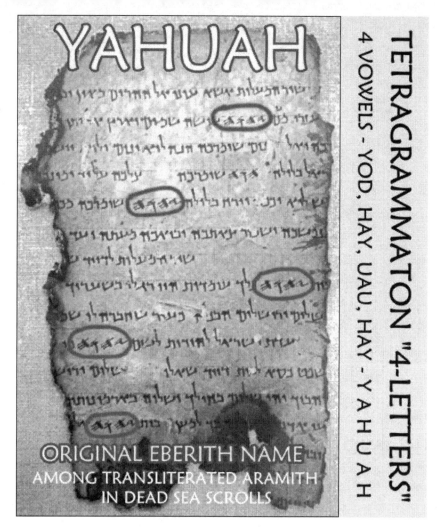

YAHUAH

ORIGINAL EBERITH NAME AMONG TRANSLITERATED ARAMITH IN DEAD SEA SCROLLS

The written language of Eberith can be transliterated using many different *scripts* (letter shapes), but the real *Eberith script* was <u>seen</u> and described by Yusef Ben MatithYahu (aka Flavius Josephus). This Yahudi historian said he saw the Name on the golden headpiece worn by the Kohen ha Gadol. He described the Name "written" in four Eberith letters, saying they were "four vowels." That headpiece was fabricated by order of Yahuah while Yisharal was in the wilderness, after the first Exodus. From that wilderness, any contact with Babel's Aramith letters (block script) as seen commonly today would be hard to imagine. Danial could read the writing on the wall because it was written in Eberith, and not the block letters the Babylonians were familiar with.

יהוה

The block letters shown here are capable of transliterating Eberith / Hebrew words, but they are the Aramith script (letters). Above we see the letters of the Name written in Aramith script. Reading right-to-left, these produce the exact sound of the Name YAHUAH. We use Latin letters for writing English, and the Yahudim that returned from Babel used the Aramith letters they learned to become proficient with. The picture below shows one authentic Eberith letter among Egyptian pictographs. Teachers are saying this is the original appearance of the letters, yet no physical evidence of the Name of Yahuah written in this way has ever been found.
The meaning of the Egyptian hieroglyphs has been transferred by equivocation; this is a specious (deceptive) Jesuit tactic.

The letters shown above are not what people think they are. We who teach the true Eberith script are concerned about the growing popularity of the Egyptian characters being promoted on the Internet. There are so many caught in the hypnotic spell of false teachings, and we need to help people discern the Truth from the myths that appear out of thin air all the time.

fossilizedcustoms.com/hyksoshoax.html

WINDOW HOOK WINDOW HAND

The real Eberith script is found in the rubble of ancient Yerushalim and Shomeron, but the block script was brought into use post-Captivity. There are bullae and pottery shards, and many seals using the real Eberith script, and these are hard evidence proving the block script is from the foreign influence of the Babylonian Captivity.

In 1947, jars were found in 11 caves at Qumran (Kumeran) which contained parchments preserving the Name.

The entire scroll of YashaYahu was found, and placed on display at the Shrine of the Book (Hekal Sefer) in Jerusalem:

THE SCROLL OF YASHAYAHU
PLACED AMONG THE DEAD SEA SCROLLS APPROXIMATELY 125 BCE
IT HAS NO NIQQUD MARKS, PHONEMES, OR SPEECH GUIDES

YOD-HAY-UAU-HAY

"YAHUAH"

The Great Isaiah Scroll

TORAH INSTITUTE RESEARCH
THE JARS PRESERVED THE NAME FOR US TODAY, AS ANY DOCUMENT HAVING THE NAME ON IT
WAS CAREFULLY HANDLED WITH GREAT RESPECT, NEVER TREATED PROFANELY

STONE FOUND IN SHOMERON

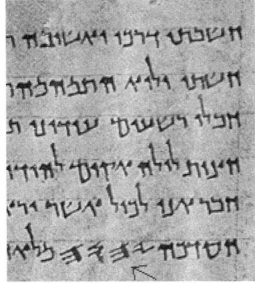

The Great Isaiah Scroll at the Hekal Sefer in Yerushalim shows the Aramith text, but this copy uses the original Eberith letters for the Name. Photos of that evidence will appear in this link:
fossilizedcustoms.com/hebrew.html

IVRIT is a Germanic / Ashkenazic distortion of the term for the **Eberith** language and script, based on the name of our forefather **Eber**.

Abrahim was Eber's great grandchild, and Eber's descendants are known as the Eberim, and today are called the Hebrews. We are progressing in understanding by taking European language alterations and unveiling how our speech became distorted. The letter BETH is never a V, but the **Nimrod Effect** (confusion) is being purified from our lips (ZekarYah 3:9).

I remind you that there were no niqqud marks (twiddlydiddles, gnats, skid -marks) anywhere until the 8th century. These speech-guides were added to the Hebrew text by Karaites at Babel. The Dead Sea Scrolls have no phonology aids, just the letters made up of vowels and consonants.

Let's review:
What is a vowel, and what is a consonant?
A **vowel** is a letter pronounced with only the breath and mouth cavity, not involving the lips, teeth, roof of the mouth, or back of the throat stopping the air flow.
A **consonant** is a letter sounded using teeth (hissing), lips and teeth (buzzing), tongue on roof of mouth as in "**D**" - "**J**"), lips (**B**, **P**, **K**), etc.
The Name of Yahuah was identified as having four vowels (not consonants) by Yusef Ben MatithYahu (aka Flavius "Josephus") as he described seeing the golden headpiece worn by the high priest.

Historical Evidence Of The Four Vowels
The Yahudi historian Flavius Josephus (real name, Yusef Ben MatithYahu) described the four vowels of the Name he personally saw inscribed on the golden headpiece worn by the High Priest: "A mitre also of fine linen encompassed his head, which was tied by a blue ribbon, about which there was another golden crown, in which was engraven the

sacred [qodesh] Name [yod-hay-uau -hay]: it consists of four vowels."

The four vowels are seen here on the Moabite Stone at the Louvre Museum in Paris, France:

fossilizedcustoms.com/fourvowels.html

Why Do We Say, "DOUBLE-U?"

The Latin letter V was a vowel, developed from the Greek upsilon. Contemporary readers see a letter for which they use the upper teeth and lower lip to make a buzzing sound, transforming it into a bilabial fricative, making it a consonant. It should be only the sound of U.

The "double-U" (VV) was invented by a typesetter in the 15th century. Later the single letter developed the buzzing we all mistake it to make.

The lips and teeth make the V into a consonant.

What Does The Word ISRAEL Mean?

A short teaching video:

https://youtu.be/1Fe8V_wmSVM

The word "ISRAEL" refers to a people, not a place. Many overlook the meaning of the phrase, ***"the LAND of Israel,"*** but the word itself has not been properly understood either. Share the above video with your friends who care about who and where the people called Israel are today. Misunderstandings continue to increase regarding the identity of Yahuah's scattered people.

The land empire of Yahuah's chosen nation has specific parameters, but its influence and *mission field* extends to the whole Earth, to the distant islands of the sea. The colonies planted 3000 years ago were the places where we have found refuge, and we are now awakening to the Covenant in all the places where we have been scattered, fulfilling prophecy (Dt. 4).

The Cherokee and Lakota tribes call the Great Spirit by His real Name:

"YAHUAH."

The Hebrew spelling of the new name given to Yaqub is **yod-shin-resh-alef-lamed** (YSHRAL in simplified Latin letters). The yod is a prefix, "to," joined with the root "SHAR," rule / ruler. The suffix is alef-lamed, AL, lofty one, referring to our Alah, Yahuah. You may recall that *prince of peace* is the English translation of the Hebrew transliteration *shar shalom.*

Words are built using their roots, often accompanied by modifying affixes called *prefixes* and *suffixes.* The meaning if the word ISRAEL is often confused because teachers misidentify word roots.

For transliterating this name, we should prefer YISHARAL, not YASHARAL.

Yasher is a root meaning upright, straight, or smooth. We can miss the meaning by mixing roots. Yisharal means *"to rule with Al."*

It refers to more than only the tribe of Yahudah, and includes the offspring of Yaqub, and those who enjoin to Yahuah through the Covenant, having the sign of the Shabath for all their generations.

Ruling Over The Flesh
Yaqub was given a new name after his encounter with the messenger of Yahuah. This teaches us to persevere in the Truth which will free us from the mind of the flesh. We have to receive the perspective of Yahuah.

The idea of overcoming brings to mind the inner mind ruling over the flesh, as we wrestle each Yom Kafar by fasting. Yaqub was a surrogate, or impostor, and was re-named Yisharal, in order that he could live-up to his new identity given to him by Yahuah. We learn from his example: to strive until we overcome all obstacles in our path to win the race. Yisharal means *"to rule with Alahim."* 2 Timothy 4:7:

"I have fought the good fight, I have finished the race, I have guarded the belief."

We wrestle to finish, to remain steadfast to the Covenant, enduring to the end through the power of He Who dwells in us.

Baruk haba baShem Yahuah!

What Is A "Black Swan" Event?
The scattering of the tribes into the nations served several purposes, and the missing Name in the translations is the big black swan event (unpredictable surprise). The unexpected discovery of the Dead Sea Scrolls is the most important archaeological find of the 20th century.

The KJV and all that follow it have taught the world the wrong name.

The scrolls at Qumran were put there over the centuries so a people yet to be created may call on the Name of Yahuah, not BEL (the LORD). Watch this video for more:

youtube: https://youtu.be/Ec2EliKxnD8

They admit in their prefaces they replaced the Name with the device "LORD," following the TRADITION of the long-standing avoidance of using it. Aduni, Bel, Kurios, Dominus, all mean LORD. This is the controversy at its core. The Christians have inherited nothing but lies and futility because their teachers have led them astray. They and their forebears have cast Yahuah's Words behind them, and yet they claim to know Him. The photo below, the Preface of the NIV, admits they removed the Name.

NIV - PREFACE

In regard to the divine name *YHWH*, commonly referred to as the *Tetragrammaton*, the translators adopted the device used in most English versions of rendering that name as "LORD" in capital letters to distinguish it from *Adonai*, another Hebrew word rendered "Lord," for which small letters are used. Wherever the two names stand together in the Old Testament as a compound name of God, they are rendered "Sovereign LORD."

Because for most readers today the phrases "the LORD of hosts" and "God of hosts" have little meaning, this version renders them "the LORD Almighty" and "God Almighty." These renderings convey the sense of the Hebrew, namely, "he who is sovereign over all the 'hosts' (powers) in heaven and on earth, especially over the 'hosts' (armies) of Israel." For readers unacquainted with Hebrew this does not make clear the distinction between *Sabaoth* ("hosts" or "Almighty") and *Shaddai* (which can also be translated "Almighty"); but the latter occurs infrequently and is always footnoted. When *Adonai* and *YHWH Sabaoth* occur together, they are rendered "the Lord, the LORD Almighty."

As for other proper nouns, the familiar spellings of the King James Version are generally retained.

The Natsarim are arising in the last days to teach the Name and Torah to the nations, and Yahusha said if they hated Him, they will hate us also. Let's not hate, but love one another, and be the light He intended us to be.

Rabbi's, Guru's, & Other Mystagogues

People learn from teachers, and their refinement comes from Yahusha.

To stay in error because that's what we have been taught, without personally testing everything, is to place our trust in man. We have to stop believing everything we hear, that's what the simple do; the clever one watches his steps. (Proverbs 14:15). There is a way that seems right to a man, but in the end leads to death. (Proverbs 14:12). Being united in Truth is what we must strive for, and compromising is not an option we should consider; that's how we got into this jam. For the 12 years I was under the tutelage of the Jesuits, I was taught to bow to images, pray to the dead, perform repetitive prayers using beads, use "holy" water, believe the sacraments would lead me to heaven, and other nonsense (like the pope is the "HOLY FATHER"). To deceive a child in his innocence to do and think such depraved behavior merits extra-special punishment from Yahuah (Mt. 18:6).

Why The World Hates The Natsarim
It's tough to watch or read the highly intolerant behavior of new teachers who jump on people for saying the wrong words. It's mostly a sign of spiritual immaturity. We should not bend to using the old traditional terms however, as some teachers do to reach larger audiences. Keep using the Scripturally correct Hebrew, and some will begin to use it. It's the stronghold in them we are dismantling, and it's done by laying the true foundation, not supporting the sandy one. They may not remember what you said, but they will remember how you made them feel, right? Yahusha left this advice to His Natsarim at Yn. 15:17-25:

"These words I command you, so that you love one another. If the world hates you, you know that it hated Me before you. If you were of the world, the world would love its own.

But because you are not of the world, but I chose you out of the world, for that reason the world hates you.

Remember the word that I said to you, 'A servant is not greater than his Aduni.' If they persecuted Me, they shall persecute you too. If they have guarded My Word, they would guard yours too. But all this they shall do to you because of My Name, because they do not know Him who sent Me. If I had not come and spoken to them, they would have no sin, but now they have no excuse for their sin. He who hates Me hates My Father as well. If I did not do among them the works which no one else did, they would have no sin. But now they have both seen and have hated both Me and My Father, but that the Word might be filled which was written in their Turah,

'They hated Me without a cause.'"

(from Yn. 15, referring to Ps. 69)

Why Should We Guard Torah?

You may never hear this in a steeple building, so listen carefully. Torah (or Turah) is the Hebrew word meaning instruction, directive, command, or teaching. Torah makes one wise.

Those who turn-away their ear from hearing Torah, even their prayers are an abomination to Yahuah (Proverbs 28:9).

Torah is wisdom; all who hate wisdom love death (read Proverbs 8:36). There is a way that seems right to a man, but it is the way of death (Proverbs 14:12). A life without guarding Yahuah's Torah is a terrible thing to waste. About the steeple buildings you see everywhere: Yahuah forbids them (Lev. 26:1), so it's not wise to keep going back to learn about Him in such a place. We cannot draw closer to Him by driving Him away from us through our rebellious behavior. Get Wisdom; read and do what He says, not the traditions handed-down to us by our fathers.

Get Wisdom; read and do what He says, not the traditions handed-down to us by our fathers. The old covenant (animal blood) is obsolete, but the Torah is eternal. We will not see Yahusha again, until we say: **"Baruk haba bashem Yahuah"** Luke 19:38-40 / Ps. 118:26

EBERITH SCRIPT
WRITTEN RIGHT-TO-LEFT
NO SPACES BETWEEN WORDS

YOD-HAY-UAU-HAY:

STEEPLE PEOPLE

BABEL IS ABOUT TO FALL - DON'T LET IT FALL ON YOU!

"The coming of the lawless one will be accompanied by the working of satan, with *every kind of power, sign, and false wonder . . .*" 2 Thess. 2:9

"Now there were also false prophets among the people, just as there will be false teachers among you. They will secretly introduce destructive heresies that even deny the Master who bought them, bringing swift destruction on themselves." 2 Pet 2:1

Many people are searching to-and-fro and knowledge is increasing exponentially. At Yahusha's return, Babel's pillars will fall. AS THE PASTORS HAVE INCREASED, SO HAS THE LAWLESSNESS

EVERY STEEPLE IS A FERTILITY PILLAR YAHUAH TOLD US NOT TO BUILD

Yahuah says He hates the **pillars** and **green trees** people erect which are adopted **fertility symbols** from pagan worship.
"Do not plant for yourself any tree as an Asherah near the altar of Yahuah your Alahim that you make for yourself. And do not set up a pillar [spire, steeple, obelisk], **which Yahuah your Alahim hates."** Dt. 16:21-22 BYNV Pastors know the origin of steeples: BABEL.

"Do not make idols for yourselves, and do not set up a carved image or a pillar for yourselves, and do not place a stone image in your land, to bow down to it, for I am Yahuah your Alahim. Guard My Shabaths and reverence My set-apart place. I am Yahuah." Leviticus 26:1-2 BYNV

Would Yahusha Want You To Teach your children to observe Constantine's Day of the Sun, or His Shabath Day? When did He tell you to bake a cake for the queen of heaven each year, make a secret wish to a genie, and blow-out candles while wearing a cone hat like a witch or sorcerer? How about fortune cookies, zodiacs, and palm-reading? Our fathers passed-down *only* futility to us:

Above photo: Page 1 of 4 - Get this whole tract and over 100 more at **www.torahzone.net**

STEEPLE PEOPLE

Every Steeple Is A Fertility Pillar
Yahuah Told Us Not To Build

Babel is about to fall; don't let it fall on you.

"The coming of the lawless one will be accompanied by the working of satan, with every kind of power, sign, and false wonder . . ."
2 Thess. 2:9

"Now there were also false prophets among the people, just as there will be false teachers among you. They will secretly introduce destructive heresies that even deny the Master who bought them, bringing swift destruction on themselves."
2 Pet 2:1

Many people are searching to-and-fro and knowledge is increasing exponentially.

At Yahusha's return, Babel's pillars will fall. As the pastors have increased, so has the lawlessness. Yahuah says He hates the **pillars** and **green trees** people erect which are adopted **fertility symbols** from pagan worship.

"Do not plant for yourself any tree as an Asherah near the altar of Yahuah your Alahim that you make for yourself. And do not set up a pillar [spire, steeple, obelisk]**, which Yahuah your Alahim hates."** (Dt. 16:21-22 BYNV)

Pastors *know*, but are not telling you;
the origin of steeples is *BABEL.*

"Do not make idols for yourselves, and do not set up a carved image or a pillar for yourselves, and do not place a stone image in your land, to bow down to it, for I am Yahuah your Alahim. Guard My Shabaths and reverence My set-apart place. I am Yahuah." Leviticus 26:1-2 BYNV

Would Yahusha want you to teach your children to observe Constantine's Day of the Sun, or His Shabath Day? When did He tell you to bake a **cake** for the queen of heaven each year, make a **secret wish** to a genie, and **blow-out candles** while wearing a cone hat like a witch or sorcerer? How about fortune cookies, zodiacs, and palm-reading? Our fathers passed-down *only* futility to us:

"Yahuah, my strength and my stronghold and my refuge, in the yom* of distress** the gentiles shall come to You from the ends of the arets and say, 'Our fathers have inherited only falsehood, futility, and there is no value in them.'"

See YirmeYahu / Jeremiah16:19
*yom: Hebrew for day   **Great Tribulation

STRANGE FIRE; YOU CAN FEEL SOMETHING IS WRONG

Pillars are **images of jealousy** (Ez. 8:1-17), the Nimrod rebellion.

Babel's fall is very near, and *steeple people are jumping-ship.*

Yahusha guarded Shabath all His life, and told us to pray our flight not be on a Shabath day (Mt. 24:20). YashaYahu (Is.) 56 and 66:23 and ZekarYah 14 mentions the Shabath, and show us that after Yahusha returns we will worship and bow to Him. Those who refuse to worship Him as He told us, but prefer to teach men's traditions in place of the Truth, are eating wormwood. The bitterness toward obedience is evident in those who refuse to acknowledge His Commandments of kindness, but we who obey His Covenant of kindness have received only a bitterness toward sin. This is why people see such a huge change in us: those who know Him have received His perspective, but those

who do not yet know Him have not.
They don't recognize their strange fire.
Ask Yahusha to help you to love His
Commandments, and *He will run to you* as the father
ran in the parable of the prodigal son.
The **old covenant** was the old priesthood and *animal
blood*, not the 10 Commandments. People who
change His Commandments and eat swine flesh are
not a source of Truth, and those without wisdom are
easily deceived by them. Some believe ***indulgences***
are real. The simple will believe anything (Prov.
14:15), trusting there is a stuffed donkey in Verona,
Italy that can give them time-off from fiery suffering in
a non-existent place called Purgatory.
How should we distinguish between the true
followers (Natsarim) and false followers of Yahusha?
Are decorated trees, pumpkins carved like faces,
and baskets filled with eggs and candy how you were
raised? All of these things are traditions handed-
down from the heathens' worship of the *host of
heaven*, and very disturbing.
Most familiar behavior taught to children and
practiced by families all around us today is the
reason people will be utterly destroyed in the **high-
temperature incineration** that is coming. Most
pastors don't warn us, not understanding 1 Kings
14:23:
**"For they also built for themselves high places,
and pillars, and Asherim on every high hill and
under every green tree."**

Do we have freedom to disobey the Commandments of Yahuah, to do things Yahuah calls an abomination? True freedom is from the *traditions of men*. Yahusha was critical of the **traditions**, not the **Torah**. Yahusha calls the teachings of men **leaven**. He was not critical of the Pharisees because they obeyed the Commandments, but because they disobeyed them and *made men's traditions their commandments.*

Yahusha's words prove this at Mt. 15:7-9:

"Hypocrites! YashaYahu (Isaiah) **rightly prophesied about you, saying, 'This people draw near to Me with their mouth, and respect Me with their lips, but their heart is far from Me. But in vain** (futility) **do they worship Me, teaching as teachings the commands of men.'"**

Many teachers of the religion of traditions need to understand that Yahuah is looking for **obedient** servants, but pastors have trained everyone to **disobey**. The pastors have grown rich teaching lies. Tradition propagates itself like leaven - until we throw it out.

Being Lured Away? Stand Firm, Yahusha Is With You

Considering the text at Romans 10:14-15, someone has to be sent to speak to those who have never heard of Yahusha. Some are expecting someone else to go, while they just sit in a pew under a steeple *listening to someone they are paying to tell them to disobey Yahuah's Commandments.*

Romans 6:16 tells us we are the servant of the one we **obey**; how can they not see this conflict?

ARE TEACHERS WANTING YOU CLOSER TO THEM, OR YAHUSHA?

How about the idea that all of us move close to one another so we can be together and stay away from the lawless unbelievers? Some want to move to **the land** now, before Yahusha regathers us. If you are being lured to move to other places just to be with other believers, beware; *David Koresh* and *Jim Jones* did that.

A time is coming when we will all live with other Torah people: **when Yahusha returns.** We are salted among the lost. If we abandon the lost where Yahusha awakened us, they will perish because we left our post. We should all be hunting for the lost, unlike pastors who are hunting for followers to hear their lies.

Instead of being where Yahusha planted us, they would have us bunched-up together and going on with our own happy goals, and be of no use to the lost. We are not sent to the healthy, but rather we are sent to the sick.

NIMROD SUNSHINE SUPERMAN – THE FIRST HUMAN DEITY

Yahusha will crush the head of the serpent, the king of Babel.

Go to the New Agers, Hindus, witches, murderers, thieves and lost Christians, and tell them Nimrod has infected their minds. Judgment day hangs right before them, and Yahusha will tread the wrong-doers in the winepress of the wrath of Yahuah very soon. His wrath is on the heads of the lawless.

Don't be lured-away by just *believing* the Word; **DO THE WORD**. Torah is like a mirror.

Don't put your Light under a basket, nor lose your saltiness. Those around you need to see a **difference** in you, or you are no longer salt. We walk as Yahusha walked. He will not wink at disobedience just because you think you believe something. Your denomination cannot deliver anyone, nor can your efforts; only His blood can justify us. Our willingness to repent and obey in His power is the first step, at our immersion, calling on Him to pardon us for our disobedience. Continuing to disobey is not an option. He gives us His Mind. Be Yahusha's Light exactly where you are planted, and teach it.

Remain a faithful servant; one day He will allow us to all be together in one place; *at the Marriage Supper of the Lamb.*

We will celebrate our marriage to the Sovereign of the Universe.

Steeple people need to come out of their slumber, and teach the Name and pledge to obey Torah. Mt. 7:20-23 says,

"So then, by their fruits you shall know them. Not everyone who says to Me, 'Master, Master,' shall enter into the reign of the shamayim, but he who is doing the desire of My Father in the shamayim. Many shall say to Me in that yom, 'Master, Master, have we not prophesied in Your Name, and cast out demons in Your Name, and done many mighty works in Your Name?' And then I shall declare to them, 'I never knew you, depart from Me, you who work lawlessness!'"

Why Humanity Is In Peril

People do not know *who* they worship.

The world is unaware that our Creator has a personal Name, and the first followers of Yahusha were quoting the prophecy that all who call on it will be delivered (Acts 2). When I opened my first copy of Scripture (an English translation), I began with the Preface.

It declared the translators had replaced the Name with a "device," and tradition was the excuse they offered. When I investigated the Hebrew script, I learned the Name is the most-used word in all Scripture, and consisted of 4 vowels. I learned what a vowel is - sounded with the breath and mouth cavity only - and I could say the Name easily: "YAHUAH." Yahusha is Yahuah (Hebrews 1:1-3), and is awakening His Natsarim to teach His Name and Word to the world before His return. He said, "I am the Vine; you are the Natsarim," the branches of His teachings.

You are unlikely to hear these things in a building with a steeple on it. A steeple is a symbol of Babel. **fossilizedcustoms.com/steeplepeople.html**

SIGNS ALL AROUND US

SHIVA & SHAKTI GENOCIDE SYMBOL
LETTER N IN ARABIC

N IS FOR NATSARIM
SHATAN KNOWS WHO HE IS AFTER CHRISTIANS ARE CALLED
NASRANI BY ARABS
NOTSRIM BY YAHUDIM
NATSARIM BY ACTS 24:5

N IS FOR NATSARIM

Yahusha named us; *"I am the Vine: you are the Natsarim."* - Yn. 15:5

In the case of what we are called by Yahusha, **Natsarim**, we take the meaning from the abstract, not the concrete. We are the descendants (off-shoots, sprouts) of His teachings, not literally roots or branches of trees or vines. The words used to identify Christians by those in the land who speak

Eberith (Hebrew), and Arabs who speak Arabic, use NOTSRIM and NASRANI even today, but Christians barely make the connection because their teachers avoid the "roots" of the first followers of Yahusha. It could lead to more questions, and their pursuit of Truth would free them from their captivity (teaching authority holding them captive). *Tradition is the infection, and Truth is the cure.* Look inside the book: **Truth Or Tradition**:

Genocidal Symbol

The letter "N" in Arabic stands for *Natsarim* when seen spray-painted on a business or home occupied by Christians. Christians need to be aware of the significance of the symbol, and that it represents the actual term the followers of Yahusha called themselves. Yahusha told them what to call themselves: "I am the Vine; you are the Natsarim." (Yn. 15:5). Outsiders first called them *Christianos* at Antioch, a term of scorn in that day.

This genocidal symbol or mark being seen all around the Internet represents a symbol of hate for Natsarim, implemented by ISIS. It's the Arabic letter "N" and takes on the appearance of a crescent & star, the symbol Islam adopted from the Hindu symbol of Shiva (the destroyer in the Hindu trinity). The Indian empire reached Arabia in 200 BCE, and many Eastern ideas, practices, and even architecture flooded into the Middle East due to the trade route called the Silk Road.

In Mosul, ISIS militants marked their letter N with spray paint. It is the crescent and star symbol, which is also the Arabic letter "N." The symbol marks all Christian property to be seized after the ultimatum. "N" is the first letter of their Arabic word for Christian,

Nasrani. In Israel, Christian tourists are all referred to as **Notzrim**.

They do not know their Hebrew roots, but are trained by traditions handed-down from antisemitic Greek and Roman cultures. The Arabs are Hebrews, being descended from Abrahim, who was a descendant of Shem (origin of word Semite: *Shemite*).

NATSARIM, NOTZRIM, NASRANI, NAZARENES

The term is used to refer to Christians by those who hate Yahusha, and also by Christians who believe the Natsarim are heretics. Read Acts 24:5, and then you will begin to see. We have been despised everywhere for the last two millennia:

"And we think it right to hear from you what you think, for indeed, concerning this sect, we know that it is spoken against everywhere."
Acts 28:22 BYNV

Yahusha can use His last Natsarim with His message of love, and transform a hater into a servant. The ISIS / Sunni movement has been using the Arabic letter for "N" to mark the homes of Christians. Yahusha said,

"ANI HA GAFEN; ATAH HA NATSARIM."
In translation it means
I am the Vine; you are the Natsarim.

YashaYahu (Is.) 52:15:
"Kings will shut their mouths . . . for they will <u>see</u> what they have not been told, and they will understand what they had not heard."

What you are about to <u>see</u> may come as a shock.

THE WHORE SITS ON THE WATERS - REVELATION 17

US CAPITOL

TEMPLE OF SHIVA & SHAKTI

SHIVA SHRINE

ROMAN BASILICA

ON YAHUAH'S TEMPLE MOUNT

HINDU SHIVA SHRINE

SHIVA TEMPLE OPENLY SHIVALING WITH SHAKTI

TORAH INSTITUTE   BOOK: WHO IS ALLAH?

SHRINE – Image Of The Destroyer

Buildings associated with ruling the masses commonly have domes. The cultures of the whole world are about to awaken to how severely they have been deceived. SHRINE - Image Of The Destroyer will upset the religious rulers, and they will hope you will not see this 30-minute video.
https://youtu.be/KqHCmTZgGvg
The video proves the linkage between all false beliefs, and how they influence billions.

What Is The Eternal Covenant?

The eternal Covenant is the Ten Commandments, teaching us how to love. The 4th one demands that we rest (no working, going out of our places, also mentioned at Acts 1:12). Heb. 4 says there remains a Shabath for the people of Alahim, and even cites that day as the seventh day. The sign of the eternal

Covenant is Yahuah's Shabath (Ez. 20:12), emphasizing both the sign itself, and the surrounding Commandments as the eternal Covenant it is found to be taken from. During the great distress, "Pray your flight will not be in winter or on yom Shabath" (Mt. 24:20).

Philosophies Of Men - a video that challenges people in the last days who believe they are "saved" or will be protected, but in fact are not even close to being in a Covenant with the Creator, Yahusha ha Mashiak.

Christians are not in a covenant of any kind, but believe they are.
Our way of life today has to be different than what people have been taught by their teachers. We have to say "Be gone" to the glittering festivals of the world (Halloween, Christmas, New Year's, Valentine's, Easter, Sun-day, steeples, popes, lying teachers), and do the Word.

Why Translations Use "LORD"
The Name has been hidden by men's teaching authorities, and exchanged for BEL (Baal). LORD is the definition of the Hebrew ADUNI, the Greek KURIOS, the Latin DOMINUS, and translations admit using a "device" to honor tradition. The Anglican Catholic KJV is the English translation based on the Latin Vulgate, and in the case of the Name Yahusha, they used the IESV christogram in the first edition. JESUS did not appear until later printings.
There is no excuse for the word LORD being used *in place of* the true Name, YAHUAH.

CHRISTOGRAMS
From Where Did IESV Originate?

Eusebius Sophronius Hieronymous (later called Jerome) produced the Latin Vulgate between 391 and 403 CE. It was considered inspired, and was the dominant translation in use by the Catholic Magisterium for over 1200 years. Eusebius used the underlined Latin letters **IESV** for the Name of Yahusha. The Name of Yahusha was encrypted as a matter of policy, using *Christograms*. In the east, it was written **IC-XC**. In the west, the letters **IHS** encrypted the Name.

The KJV is Anglican Catholic and based on the Latin Vulgate.

The underlined letters **IESV** is the smoking gun; the Latin Vulgate used it for over 1200 years as a substitute for the true Hebrew Name, Yahusha. Another embarrassing fact is how the translators admit they removed the Name of the Creator and inserted "LORD" in all-caps tor represent (eliminate) the Name. This is admitted in the preface (provided in better editions).

Many different kinds of misunderstandings have come through the KJV.

At Mt. 26:17, the *"On the first day of unleavened bread"* (the 15th of the month as Yahusha was in the tomb wrapped-up), the KJV claims the disciples asked Him where He wanted them to prepare for the Passover (always on the 14th). He is the Passover, but Anglican Catholics don't have one, nor do they know when it is if asked. Other English translations have followed these errors, and you will find them in every popular version.

BYNV:
A Natsarim Version Of The Scripture Of Truth
As truth-seekers have read the BYNV, they have shared with me that they receive the impression it is

Yahusha's interpretation of His Word carried into English. What He really intended to say has been held until the prophecy He made concerning the end could be fulfilled. The babbling lip (foreign language) the world shares is English, and it was taught to them by reading the KJV. What the KJV has removed is now being shouted from the rooftops: **The Name of Yahuah.**

Each moment of the last 35 years He was teaching me how differently men's teachings of what He intended to say was twisted, resulting in a bitterness toward obedience. All they needed was a way of looking at Paul's writings with a darkened eye. After Peter warned us of the coming fiery judgment of disobedient mankind, he writes this:

"So then, beloved ones, looking forward to this, do your utmost to be found by Him in peace, spotless and blameless, and reckon the patience of our Aduni as deliverance, as also our beloved brother Paul wrote to you, according to the wisdom given to him, as also in all his letters, speaking in them concerning these matters, in which some are hard to understand, which those who are untaught and unstable twist to their own destruction, as they do also the other Scriptures. You, then, beloved ones, being forewarned, watch, lest you also fall from your own steadfastness, being led away with the delusion of the lawless, but grow in the favor and knowledge of our Aduni and Deliverer Yahusha Mashiak. To Him be the esteem both now and to a yom that abides. Aman." 2 Peter 3:14-18 BYNV

The Name of Yahuah was, is, and will be continually avoided by those who are afraid of offending other human beings. His Name is like a burning fire in my bones, and I cannot hold it back (YirmeYahu 20:9 agrees).

We live in the Information Age, but I'm offering another name for it: the "I'm offended Age." We have to realize we have offended Yahuah for calling Him Aduni, Kyrios, Dominus, and LORD, because all these transliterations pertain to BEL (the storm deity of the Kananites) by definition. The first, second, and third Commandments are violated if we call on another, misuse, or destroy His Name. YashaYahu 42:8: "I am Yahuah; that is My Name, and I will not give My esteem to another, nor My praise to another."

A Video: A last days message from Kabaquq 2:1-4 entitled:
Doers Of The Word *(not hearers only, deceiving yourselves):* **https://youtu.be/BnWq7QY-FEs**

Phyllis joins me in this video to make the point that Natsarim have a different perspective about obedience than Christians have. We have received Yahusha, Who brings us a love for His Commandments.
The Sunday-JESUS pastors are bitter toward obedience of Yahusha's Commandments, but they have received a love for men's traditions. They practice all the re-purposed pagan celebrations, and even know about their origins. Most of them claim the pagan feasts were cleansed, and now honor their JESUS, seared in their consciences as with a hot iron. Let's see what the Word of Yahuah says, and make every effort to be found doing (practicing) what He wants.

They Will Call For Peace and Safety

Peace and safety, then sudden destruction; of what? Read 1 Thessalonians 5:3.
As the World Order plans unfold, the Sovereign of Esteem (Yahuah) is about to stand up. Yes, it's true; the beast is the World Order, the mother of harlots (Babel).

Fallen! Fallen!
The mother of harlots will fall when Yahusha returns to meet His bride. Revelation calls her Babel, the original teaching authority still running the world order through the three estates: clergy, nobility, and laity, given her authority by the dragon.
Because the dragon will be bound for 1000 years, the reign of Babel will evaporate, and Yahusha's reign will reign forever and ever (with a brief head-stomping of the dragon after His first 1000 years).
fossilizedcustoms.com/beast.html

Evidence Of Our Belief
The Hebrew word for "belief" (AMUNAH) is not the blind Greek concept of only knowing or thinking something to be true. It becomes expressed in the person in such a way there is no doubt about what they believe. It is expressed by their actions (lived-out), or "heeded." To hear and obey is the point Yaqub (James) made when he wrote (1:22):
"Be doers of the Word, not hearers only, deceiving yourselves."
The just will live by belief (AMUNAH - Romans 1:17, Hab. 2:4, Gal. 3:11).
With Yahusha's Mind in us, we overcome the deception that obeying is bitter and disgusting. Obedience is only disgusting to those who put that idea into our minds. Until we surrender to Yahusha's

Truth, we remain captives, imprisoned by the teaching authority promoting doctrines of demons. *"If you abide (live-out) My Word, you are truly My talmidim, and you will know the Truth, and the Truth will set you free."* Yn. 8:31-32

Overcoming Strongholds & False Ideas
We are the descendants of Abrahim for one reason: we do what Abrahim did (see Yahukanon / Jn. 8:39-40). Yahusha responded to those who claimed Abrahim as their father, and also Alahim to be their father. Their fruits revealed who their father was, and Yahusha explained it to them. We look at the fruit to identify the tree, and we accept the wild branches grafted-in. We are created from one blood; all races and languages who carry the sign of the Covenant are welcome (Shabath), but winds of teachings are stirring people to spread malice and slander toward one another. Due to the increase in lawlessness, the love of many has grown cold.

"But the yom of Yahuah shall come as a thief in the lailah, in which the shamayim shall pass away with a great noise, and the elements shall melt with intense heat, and the arets and the works that are in it shall be burned up. Seeing all these are to be destroyed in this way, what kind of people ought you to be in qodesh behaviour and reverence, looking for and hastening the coming of the yom of Alahim, through which the shamayim shall be destroyed, being set on fire, and the elements melt with intense heat! But according to His promise we wait for a renewed shamayim and a renewed arets in which obedience dwells." 2 Peter 3:10-13 (BYNV)

Remembering The Death Of A Fellow Servant

A fellow teacher has fallen asleep.

Brad Scott's life is a good memory I will always cherish. Natsarim do not grieve like the rest of mankind, who have no hope.

"And we know that all things work together for good to those who love Yahuah, to those who are called according to His purpose. Because those whom He knew beforehand, He also established beforehand to be conformed to the likeness of His Son, for Him to be the first-born among many brothers. And whom He established beforehand, these He also called, and whom He called, these He also declared right. And whom He declared right, these He also esteemed. What then shall we say to this? If Yahuah is for us, who is against us? . . . . .

Truly, He who did not spare His own Son, but delivered Him up on behalf of us all – how shall He not, along with Him, freely give us all else?

Who shall bring any charge against Yahuah's chosen ones? It is Yahuah who is declaring right. Who is he who is condemning? It is Mashiak who died, and furthermore is also raised up, who is also at the right hand of Yahuah, who also makes intercession for us. Who shall separate us from the love of the Mashiak? Shall pressure, or distress, or persecution, or scarcity of food, or nakedness, or danger, or sword? As it has been written, 'For Your sake we are killed all yom long, we are reckoned as sheep of slaughter.' But in all this we are more than overcomers through Him who loved us. For I am persuaded that neither death nor life, nor messengers nor principalities nor powers, neither the present nor the future, nor height nor depth, nor any other creature, shall be able to separate us from the love of Yahuah which is in Mashiak Yahusha our Aduni." - Romans 8:28-39

Teachers are not helping us do something very important. Read this sentence slowly, and meditate on what it is saying to all of us:
Psalm 102:18: ***"This is written so a generation to be created may call on the Name of Yah."***
We do not see the Name written in very many translations, so we have to dig for the Pearl of Great Price until we find it.
The four Eberith / Hebrew letters (Tetragrammaton) of the Name of Yahuah are all vowels, and the third letter is a U. We hear it in hallel U Yah, yasha YahU, NetanyahU, Uyiqara (the Eberith word for the 3rd book of Mushah), and YahUsha. This sixth letter U was adopted into the Greek script as UPSILON. The V we know today uses the lower lip and upper teeth to produce a buzzing sound, making it a consonant. The marks called niqqud vowel-marks are an 8th century invention of the Masoretes (traditionalists), a sect of Anan's Karaite movement. These are not found in any of the Dead Sea Scrolls, since vowels are written letters.
There's no **V** sound in Eberith, Greek, or Latin; the shape **V** was the Latin letter sounded as our letter U. Some misunderstood words this vowel is found in are **V**ENUS and GLADI**V**S, and they should be U̲ENUS and GLADIU̲S. The symbol we call the "**double-U**" was invented by a type-setter in the 15th century to save space and time. He made two V-shaped Latin letters into one metal piece of type, producing the new letter "**W**" (double-U).
Vowel: only the mouth cavity is used; no lips, no lips or tongue on teeth, no gutteral stops (no buzzing or clicking either). **fossilizedcustoms.com/w.html**

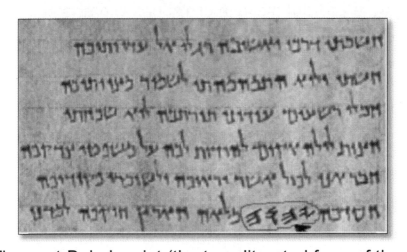

The post-Babel script (the transliterated form of the Eberith script) is abundantly represented among the Dead Sea Scrolls, while the true Eberith script is found as well. No speech guides (gnats or skid-marks) are found in any of the DSS. The physical evidence is so compelling (and offensive to tradition) its very existence has to be re-interpreted, hidden, and controlled by authoritarian teaching authorities such as the Jesuit scroll team and Ecole Biblique at Jerusalem. The Name is the centerpiece of their controversy. Their control over phonology is ending quickly as knowledge increases. The **Great Isaiah Scroll** on display in Jerusalem's Hekal Sefer (Shrine of the Book) is one of the most compelling witnesses of the true Eberith script for the Tetragrammaton before the eyes of the whole world.

GOT SACRAMENTS?
Are Those Sacraments Working Out For You?
What if Yahusha were to tell us how contemporary Christian teachers are doing? Would things look to Him as being close to what He intended?
The teachers call on no name He would recognize, nor a Shabath, or festivals He observed; only

traditions inherited from ancient pagan practices. Could we possibly fall any further away from our first love (Torah)? He removed our lampstand (menorah) long ago, and we fell for Constantine's solar crux as the symbol he worshiped. The way of Truth has been maligned, and no one seems to be aware of it (2 Peter 2:2).

There are no sacraments mentioned in the Scripture of Truth, nor any other path to uprightness trusting in Yahusha's offering of His blood (the renewed Covenant), and with His indwelling we are circumcised in our hearts to love obeying the Ten Commandments, the eternal Covenant. You're not going to fall for the traditions handed-down by *men's teachings*, are you?

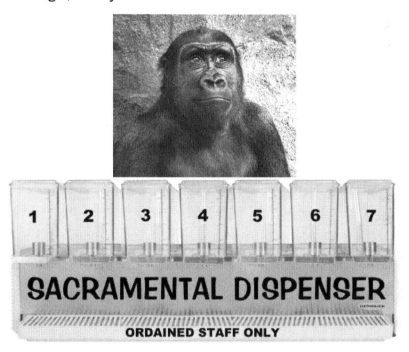

SACRAMENTAL DISPENSER

ORDAINED STAFF ONLY

"For I am more stupid than anyone, And do not have the understanding of a man. And I have not learned wisdom That I should know the knowledge of the Qodesh One. Who has gone up

to the shamayim and come down? Who has gathered the wind in His fists? Who has bound the mayim in a garment? Who established all the ends of the arets? What is His Name, And what is His Son's Name, If you know it? Every Word of Aluah is tried; He is a shield to those taking refuge in Him. Do not add to His Words, Lest He reprove you, and you be found a liar. Two things I have asked of You – Deny them not to me before I die: Remove falsehood and a lying word far from me; Give me neither poverty nor riches; Feed me my portion of bread; Lest I become satisfied and deny You, And say, "Who is Yahuah?"
Proverbs 30:2-9 BYNV

Can Belief Without Works Save You?

A day is coming, burning like a furnace - Malaki 4:1-6. Yahuah's burning wrath will not be quenched or held back because a person only "believes" in Him. He's looking for active, living obedience. Even demons believe in Him. Many will be destroyed as we watch their eyes melt in their sockets for ignoring Yahuah's eternal Covenant sign, Shabath (ZekarYah 14:12), for eating the flesh of pigs (YashaYahu 66:17), and they will die screaming by the tens of thousands (Ps. 91:7-16) - all because they refused to obey, nor accept His help in obeying and understanding. It will be even worse for the fallen ones who deceived and misled all mankind. He's awakening a relatively small flock to bring attention to what His will is before He returns to reign. Amus 3:7 - "For Aduni Yahuah does no matter unless He reveals His secret to His servants the prophets."

Yahusha's true followers are being refined and sealed in His Name to guide many to obedience (Danial 12). In an instant, at the moment He shouts, we will be clothed with immortality, and those not obeying will suffer sudden, catastrophic events so extremely devastating they will cry out curses at the one they have been misled to worship by their teachers, impostors who masquerade as messengers of light (2 Korinthians 11:14).

What we believe as correct or incorrect is mostly influenced by what we've been told to apply or ignore by men's philosophies, but Scripture is always correct. Those who overcome what men have taught them to obey (traditions) are rejected as false teachers, just as Yahusha was rejected by the teaching authority in place 2000 years ago.
Many are being refined, and leading many to obedience, because the end of days is closing in quickly. Our hope is to be counted in the group who have unwrinkled garments, clean and white from the washing of the Word, Yahusha.
Belief, without works, is dead.
We have to be *doers* of the Word, not hearers only; our belief is expressed by what we do, not what we think. The Greek mindset focuses on the mental aspects of knowledge, but Yahuah seeks outward obedience.
Our expression is not just words, but actions. This is the point of the parable of the man who had two sons. Which one of the two sons did his father's will? It was not the one who said he would do it, but rather the one who actually did it.

Question: What delivers us?
Answer: Yahusha's blood.
The dividing wall built by men's philosophies is removed, as Yahusha's blood delivers all who trust in Him, not the old covenant: animal blood and its

priesthood (Heb. 8:13, Eph. 3). His life is reflected in our behavior: because He dwells in us, we bear His fruits.

Ecclesiastes 12:13-14, Malaki 4:1-6, YashaYahu 25, and Revelation 12:17 (and many others) describe the outcome of refusing to obey the eternal Covenant, our wedding vows with our Creator.

Mt. 19:16-30 discusses obedience to the Ten Commandments, as does 1 Yn. 2:4.

Scripture is not divided into an old testament and new testament, but rather it is a seamless message calling all who will obey to eternal life.

Here is a question for the lawless:

"But to the lawless Alahim said, 'What right have you to recite My laws, or take My Covenant in your mouth, while you hated instruction and cast My Words behind you?'"

Psalm 50:16-17 BYNV Receiving a love for the Truth is paramount; disobedience shows we serve another master (Romans 6:16).

Animal Blood: The Old Covenant

The old covenant was written on a scroll and placed beside the ark (Dt. 31:26). It required animal blood, and the old priesthood. Yahusha fulfilled and replaced that priesthood (Hebrews 8:13).

Yahusha came to destroy the works of the devil; He did not come to destroy His Commandments, which teach us how to love.

Love has grown cold due to lawlessness, not lawfulness. Pastors have made obedience bitter to all who listen to them; but it is sin (disobedience) the Natsarim are exposing, and the dragon is enraged (Rev. 12:17).

Days Of Distress Shortened For The Chosen

The inhabitants have ignored Malaki 4 and YashaYahu 24, but the chosen will understand: *"And woe to those who are pregnant and to those who are nursing children in those Yomim! And pray that your flight does not take place in winter or on the Shabath. For then there shall be great distress, such as has not been since the beginning of the world until this time, no, nor ever shall be. And if those Yomim were not shortened, no flesh would be delivered, but for the sake of the chosen ones those Yomim shall be shortened. If anyone then says to you, 'Look, here is the Mashiak!' or 'There!' do not believe. For malicious Mashiaks and malicious prophets shall arise, and they shall show great signs and wonders, so as to lead astray, if possible, even the chosen ones. See, I have forewarned you. So if they say to you, 'Look, He is in the desert!' do not go out; or 'Look, He is in the inner rooms!' do not believe. For as the lightning comes from the east and shines to the west, so also shall the coming of the Son of Adam be."* Mt. 24:19-27 BYNV

Truth Is Reality
Pastors teach tradition, not Truth, so their hearers are confused (YashaYahu 9:16).
There is no forgiveness without the offering of blood. The old (temporary) Covenant offered the blood of **animals**, and was imperfect.

Old / Temporary Atonement Covenant:
This was hand-written on a **scroll**, placed beside the ark, and involved animal blood offered through the now-obsolete priesthood (compare Dt. 31:26 with Hebrews 8:13).

It was unable to redeem completely, being imperfect. It pointed to the redemption plan, the shadow of things to come, the blood of the **Lamb of Alahim**.

Remade / Permanent Redemption Covenant:
The Ten Words remain unchanged (YirmeYahu 31), written in stone by Yahuah's finger (inside the ark). These are now written on our hearts (circumcised) by the indwelling Ruach of Yahusha for those **trusting in His blood** for their complete redemption, pledged in immersion to obey His eternal Covenant. (compare Mt. 26:28, 1Pet. 3:20-22, and Hebrews 10:16, 1Yn. 2:4). Because He lives in us, we obey Him. Yahuah is Yahusha. He is the Vine, we are the Natsarim.

What does Yahusha want?
Obedience, what else? We are servants of the one we obey, and we are not the servants of the one we disobey. (Romans 6:16)
Yaqub (James) 1:19 tells us we need to be quick to listen, slow to speak, and slow to anger. When the Ten Commandments are lived-out, they call to us in the night, and protect us in the day.
By meditating on them day and night, they become a way of life. Psalm 25:14 tells us Yahuah confides in those who fear Him, and He makes His Covenant known to them. Pastors need to teach them, and parents need to train their children and grandchildren by them. *The Way of Peace they do not know.* (Romans 3:17, YashaYahu 59:8)
The Torah will go forth from Tsiun after Yahusha returns. Pastors have trained the world to be bitter toward Torah, not bitter toward sin. Kolossians 2:8 warned us about this.

People crowd together under their steeples (BEL towers, objects Yahuah forbids, Lev. 26:1), subjecting their minds to a weekly therapy session in eisegesis. This trains them to regard obeying the Ten Commandments as more than undesirable, while receiving the philosophies of men which guide them to disobey, and lead them toward eternal destruction. The Torah is the way of life, wisdom, and Truth. Yahusha only gives His Spirit to those who obey Him (Acts 5:32).
Yahusha's Natsarim are here to expose the darkness. Join us!
Google: Yahusha; I am the Vine, you are the Natsarim.

What Is The Creator Waiting For?
Your challenge is not what the pastors tell you it is. What would Yahuah* do if the world stopped being lawless, and every person would read the Ten Commandments each morning and examined themselves for which one is the most difficult?
"If only they had obeyed My Torah (instructions)." (see YashaYahu 48:18, Dt. 5:29, Mal. 4:1-6).
Let's DO THE WORD everyone, and test Him in this.
He is only waiting for this moment to arrive!
fossilizedcustoms.com/ten.html
*Yahuah: transliteration of the 4 Hebrew vowels used 6,823 times in Scripture (yod-hay-uau-hay). Mt. 12:37 – Yahusha's Words matter. Love one another with your words.

All Scripture Is Alahim-Breathed
Let's test our own ignorance first:
Question: "*Why does Matthew 27:9 attribute the prophecy to Jeremiah when it is from Zechariah?*"

The answer that I agree with more than any other follows, with corrected terms in parentheses, from gotquestions.org *[quote]*:

"The (message) of Matthew says that the (Sanhedrin) took the blood money that Judas Iscariot had returned to them and used it to buy a potter's field to bury strangers in.

Their action was a fulfillment of prophecy: **"Then what was spoken by Jeremiah the prophet was fulfilled: 'They took the thirty pieces of silver, the price set on him by the people of Israel, and they used them to buy the potter's field, as (Yahuah) commanded me'"** *(Matthew 27:9–10).*
The prophecy Matthew alludes to regarding 30 pieces of silver is most likely from Zechariah 11:12–13, which reads, "I told them, 'If you think it best, give me my pay; but if not, keep it.' So they paid me thirty pieces of silver. And (Yahuah) said to me, 'Throw it to the potter'—the handsome price at which they valued me! So I took the thirty pieces of silver and threw them to the potter at the house of (Yahuah)."

. . . Why would Matthew appear to attribute the prophecy of the 30 pieces of silver to Jeremiah instead of Zechariah?

The most likely answer is found in the structure of the (TaNaK).
The (TaNaK) is divided into three sections called the Law, Writings, and Prophets. (Yahusha) refers to these divisions in Luke 24:44. The collection of the Prophets began with the book of Jeremiah. The scrolls were sometimes referred to by the name of the first book, which in the case of the Prophets would be Jeremiah.

*When Matthew says that "Jeremiah says," he means the **prophecy** was found in the "Jeremiah Scroll."*

The best solution is probably found in the understanding of how the (Natsarim writers) spoke of the parts of Scripture. It is also interesting that the one (message) writer to note this event was Matthew, who had previously worked as a tax collector. He would have been very familiar with monetary transactions and likely well aware of the purchase price of the Field of Blood, which he immediately connected with Zechariah's prophecy of 30 pieces of silver. Matthew used this connection to show one of the ways the coming of (Yahusha) fulfilled numerous predictions in the (TaNaK), affirming (Yahusha) as the true Messiah." [end quote]

Baruk haba baShem Yahuah!

ORIGIN OF THE WORD BIBLE
Why Natsarim should not use the word BIBLE
Where did the word BIBLE come from?
We stand firmly on the Word of Yahuah, not the passing words of men. For example, 2 Tim. 3:16-17 says: **"All Writing [graphe] is breathed by Yahuah and profitable for teaching, for reproof, for setting straight, for instruction in obedience, that the man of Yahuah might be fitted, equipped for every good work."**
The Writing Paul is speaking of in this context is the Scriptures of Truth (Danial 10:21, KETHAB AMATH). Yahuah does not call His Word BIBLE, that's a pagan deity BYBLIA.
The Greeks adopted their term for "parchment" from the name of the city BYBLOS named after the deity Byblia.

Danial 10:21 calls the writings "KETHAB AMATH" - meaning *scripture of truth*, not BIBLE.

BIBLE is not an inspired word in the scripture of truth, but is from the Greek language. What we would call "paper" today was a main export from a city called Byblos. It produced papyrus. The city was named after a female fertility deity whose temple was there, Byblia (worshiped by Romans by the name Uenus). Natsarim are being trained to restore the pure lip to call on Yahuah, and avoid taking the names of foreign deities on our lips (Exodus 23:13).

Syncretism makes stuff mean other stuff.

We seek to do the things that are pleasing to Yahusha.

How Did The Day Of The Sun Become The Christian Day To Rest?

The first to state his case seems right, and there is a way that seems right.

Study reveals the difference between truth and tradition. We've inherited nothing lies and futility because the traditions of our fathers are taught, not Yahuah's Words.

We discern the spirit of error in the word Sunday when another comes to question us. Truly, we have been led astray by men's philosophies, who have removed the sign of the eternal Covenant, the 7th day (Heb. 4, Ez. 20).

Yahusha told us to pray our flight not be on the Shabath (Mt. 24:20) during the great distress of nations. The pressure on converts to divert from the first Natsarim assemblies by the Fiscus Judaicus. The Edict of Constantine in 313 CE made resting on the 7th day incur the death penalty, and resting was ordered on dies Solis (day of the Sun) in all the cities of the Roman Empire. The dogma to rest for all

Christians became compulsory at the council of Laodicea (circa 370 CE). The sign of the eternal Covenant (Ez. 20:12) was severed completely, and true worshipers literally had to run to the hills. Natsarim were valley dwellers (Waldensians, those living between the walled valleys), and also known as Huguenots, and Albigenses. We worship every day, because worship means obedience, and we become good at it with practice, and the indwelling guidance of Yahusha's Spirit. People are trained to disobey, and acquire a bitterness toward obedience, not a bitterness toward sin. Because they taught error, people have grown more lawless with each generation, and their teachers will be held responsible.

ARE YOU LUKEWARM?
Get out of the circus, and join the Natsarim, because you've been taught to disobey Yahuah, and follow men's traditions instead, making a covenant with death. Yahusha said, "I am the Vine, you are the Natsarim."
We are spoken against everywhere (Acts 28:22). We guard (obey) the Commandments, and teach them. We have no agenda other than to warn those who are searching for the Truth to repent and obey the written Word, trusting in the blood of Yahusha instead of animal blood (the old covenant), and be immersed calling on Him to forgive us for our crimes against Him.

You will no longer be luke-warm, He will give His Spirit only to those who obey Him (Acts 5:32). If you stay as you are, He will have no place for you when He returns.

You will be one of the Natsarim, not a *Christianos* (cretin, idiot; we were were first referred to as Christianos at Antioch). Read what we were really called at Acts 24:5. The Christians don't know this, but they are called NOTSRIM by Israelis, NASRANIS by Arabs, and we who follow Yahusha are called NATSARIM (branches) among themselves. Those who know Yahusha obey the Commandments; those who don't obey need to find out what He calls them at 1 Yn. 2:4.

One Name is turning the <u>world</u> upside down . . . again. (really, it's turning it right-side-up).
What happened at Mt. Karmel (1 Kings 18, Acts 17) is significant. Now a global plague (2 Kron 7, YashaYahu 48) together with the outpouring of Yahuah's Ruach on both men and women (Yual 2:28, Acts 2:17) is working to fulfill Danial 12 - the end of days. *Baruk haba baShem Yahuah!*

Is Alazar (Lazarus) **Among Us?**
When people ask me to explain myself, I remind them to not be concerned with one another's mission, but follow the purpose Yahusha has given for them to follow Him. Peter had known young Alazar, the brother of Miryam and Martha, the disciple whom Yahusha loved, and had raised from the tomb. After Yahusha told him how he would die, Peter wondered about Alazar, and if he would ever die.
"Peter turned and saw that the disciple whom Yahusha loved was following them. (This was the one who had leaned back against Yahusha at the supper and had said, "Lord, who is going to betray you?") When Peter saw him, he asked, 'Master, what about him?'

Yahusha answered, 'If I want him to remain alive until I return, what is that to you? You must follow me.' Because of this, the rumor spread among the believers that this disciple would not die. But Yahusha did not say that he would not die; he only said, 'If I want him to remain alive until I return, what is that to you?' This is the disciple who testifies to these things and who wrote them down. We know that his testimony is true." Yn. 20:20-24

Untwisting False Eschatology

The prophecy made by Yahusha at Mt. 16:28 is impossible, but what is impossible for men is possible for Yahusha (Luke 18:27) if we know Who He really is. Philip asked to see the Father. "Have I been with you so long, yet you have not recognized Me, Philip?" (Yn. 14:9)

At Mt. 16:28 He told them, "Some standing here will not taste death until they see the Son of Adam coming in His reign."

Mankind is more likely to accept what is deemed possible. From a preterist's standpoint, the alternative is too fantastic to comprehend.

Yahusha made the prophecy concerning Yahukanon remaining until He returns (Yn. 21:22) after His Resurrection, so Mt. 16:28 could not have been fulfilled by the *transfiguration* (Mt. 17).

Many of us want to draw closer to Yahusha to know Him by His real Name, and it's not wrong to help others learn how the traditions of our fathers are leading us away from Truth. To live with a tradition we acknowledge to be wrong, yet practice it because we get results, makes us like the priests of BEL in the days of AliYahu. Izebel was eaten by dogs, and

Ahab's male descendants were cut-off, all because they deceived their people concerning the correct Name. If BEL (LORD) is Alahim, serve him; but if Yahuah is Alahim, serve Him. Yahuah is Yahusha, the Alef-Tau, Al Shaddai (Rev. 1:8, Heb. 1:1-3).

Are _You_ The Prophet, Or Is It Yahusha Who Speaks?

Prophecy is marvelous to think about, and really it's Yahusha Himself in us quickening our thoughts about Him and what He's done, and what He plans to do. The Spirit of prophecy is the testimony of Yahusha, both speaking to us from the prophets' writings, and actively speaking in us. He's the Prophet, we're the vessels He uses. Once, Yahuah used a donkey to speak to a man known to be a prophet!

YESHUA or YAHUSHA?

As a name, the diminutive form for the son of Nun is found once at NekemYah 8:17, spelled YOD-SHIN-UAU-AYIN (YSHUA). In 216 other places the spelling is YOD-HAY-UAU-SHIN-AYIN (YAHUSHA), a transformative word invented by Mushah for Husha, first used at Numbers 13:16.
The word YESHUA is a word meaning deliver, rescue, or save. The acronym YESHU (seen as JESCHU in the Talmud) stands for yermak shmo uzikro, "may his name be blotted out."
Let's use the one Name given to us for our Deliverer, and never deny it: YAHUSHA, meaning:
"I am your Deliverer."

What is His Name, and what is His Son's Name if you can tell? (Prov. 30:4) Do you sometimes feel you are "always learning, but never able to come to a knowledge of the Truth?" (2 Timothy 3:7)

The Name is so easy to understand, but most reject YAHUSHA, the one Hebrew Name we must be immersed in as they say, *"I don't speak Hebrew, besides, He knows who I mean."* They don't speak Greek or Latin either, but prove the words of Maimonides;

"Men like the opinions to which they have been accustomed from their youth; they defend them, and shun contrary views; and this is one of the things that prevents men from finding truth, for they cling to the opinion of habit."
Guide For The Perplexed

Other names that are Hebrew they will accept (Adam, Mikal, Abraham, Seth, Esau, and dozens of others), yet in spite of not speaking Hebrew, they manage fine.

Human traditions are the most insidious enemy of the Truth. The Truth is spreading into the whole world, and we are saying what Yahusha told us we would be saying just before He comes to burn the weeds and gather the wheat.

What Is The Old Covenant?
The misunderstanding most have is "which Torah" are we freed from? The torah we are free from, fulfilled by Yahusha, was the old covenant requiring the covering of sin with animal blood, and the old priesthood (see Dt. 31:26). It was the torah written on a scroll, and placed beside the ark, as the text says. The eternal Torah was written on our hearts by submitting to Yahusha, our trusting in His blood, which now saves us through the observance of His Covenant with His indwelling (Paraklita). Hebrews 8:13 reflects this change in Torah, and the

priesthood, but the world is taught disobedience, and trained to sin.

TRINITY CONFUSION

Trinity confusion is a world-wide form of mass hypnosis, practically identical to what is called the "Mandela Effect" in modern times. It has slowly overcome the minds of many millions who go to steeples each week for their therapy session in eisegesis. To help people awaken to exegesis, Revelation 1:8, Acts 20:28, Barashith 2:15, Barashith 22:7, and Yn. 1:29 could be in there somewhere to show us what Yahuah did in (and through) the Seed we know as our only Redeemer (YashaYahu 43:11). If Yahuah is three, why did He not tell us if we needed to know it? Why are teachers teaching about the animals in the sky (heavenly host / zodiac) as if we need to know about them? Why are so many unknowingly following the patterns of Nimrod, Shemiramis, and Tammuz, adopting Nimrod's reincarnation triune mythology, inherited by all the ancient cultures, and expressed in Hinduism's Brahma, Uishnu, and Shiba? Trinities caused the whole world to go mad-drunk, and originated in Babel, the golden cup Yahuah allowed the nations to drink from for their disobedience (YirmeYahu 51:7). If you need any research material, check out **fossilizedcustoms.com/trinity.html**

Mythological Trinity

The word trinity is unused in Scripture, but this does not hold-back the teachers of confusion. They hold to traditions handed-down to them, keeping them away from understanding Truth. 1 Timothy 1:7 describes the teachers' problem. They have turned aside to myths.

NIMROD TRINITIES EXPRESSED IN PERSIAN, CELTIC, HINDU, AND EGYPTIAN CULTURES

The founder of Catholicism embraced many Hindu myths, and his Nicene Creed is the evidence of how the trinity became so much a part of the circus culture around us. Here is the first page of a tract available as a PDF (see back page):

TURNED ASIDE TO MYTHS

WHAT ARE THEY, WHO'S DOING IT, AND WHAT COULD POSSIBLY GO WRONG?

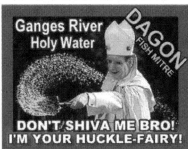 

Ganges River Holy Water — DAGON FISH MITRE — DON'T SHIVA ME BRO! I'M YOUR HUCKLE-FAIRY!

WHY DOES CHRISTIANITY LOOK LIKE SUN WORSHIP?

Sound doctrines are all now replaced by traditions of men. Futility, lies, and myths have filled the earth with customs people embrace as familiar, and the Truth has become thought of as evil. Paul wrote of these things to Timothy: **"Proclaim the Word! Be urgent in season, out of season. Correct, warn, appeal, with all patience and teaching. For there shall be a time when they shall not bear sound teaching, but according to their own desires, they shall heap up for themselves teachers tickling the ear, and they shall indeed turn their ears away from the Truth, and be turned aside to myths."** 2Timothy 4:2-4

A myth is a widely-held belief, among these are sacraments, holy water, transubstantiation, Sun-day, Trinities, celibacy, image worship, popes, nuns, monks, steeples, obelisks, wreaths, lent, chants, special days, prayers to the dead, indulgences, pilgrimages, stigmatas, Easter egg hunts, Dec. 25th Solstice birth, Santa, elves, trees in homes, monstrances, bells, and all forms of fertility patterns of Babel.

TEACHING AS TEACHINGS THE COMMANDS OF MEN

Luke reports for us in Acts about many events spanning about 32 years after the death and resurrection of Yahusha. He describes many of the challenges faced by his fellow traveler and convert we know as Paul. Paul was formerly known as Shaul, who had been given authority by the Sanhedrin to arrest the Natsarim (branches) in the assemblies found to be uttering Yahuah's Name, which they called blasphemy. Shaul was confronted by Yahusha in Person on his way to Damascus. Paul was gifted with skills and mentored by Gamaliel. Gamaliel was the grandson of the noble Torah teacher Hillel. Paul was able to speak to anyone who would listen, and was not intimidated in the least by any lawyers, judges, sophists, governors or kings.

PAGE 1 OF 4 - GET ENTIRE TRACT: TORAHZONE.NET

The Mysteries: Doctrines Of Demons

The trinity doctrine is very old, the template is based on Babel's Nimrod, Semiramis, and Tammuz.

The trinity is expressed in the AUM (OM) symbol of Hinduism. This mystery religion babbled the names of Nimrod's family as Brahma (creator), Uishnu (preserver), and Shiba (destroyer). Nimrod was believed to have ascended into the heavens as the Sun. His rebirth was celebrated on the winter Solstice, making him the first human mighty one to be worshiped, opposing Yahuah.

Nimrod's triune family is the origin of all reincarnation mythologies, resulting in ancestor worship. Nimrod was thought of as being "re-born" in his child, Tammuz). Here is a link to another video on one of my youtube channels which I did with Mark Davidson several years ago, and it gives more details.

There's a reason the trinity idea is promoted:
to disguise the true identity of Yahusha.
https://youtu.be/SR29lCqpB88

GOSSIP IS MURDER

Gossiping: Not A Fruit Of The Spirit
fossilizedcustoms.com/gossip.html

There are goats, and there are sheep, but both belong to Yahusha. Aim at being a sheep (following only Yahusha), but the goats among us give us a head-butting because it seems they are also necessary to train us and keep us humble.
Without persecution, we would never learn humility. The pain we feel when persecuted we would never inflict on another; they do not know what they are doing.
To share in the sufferings of Yahusha is a wonderful thing, but forgiving those who persecute us is how He shapes our hearts to endure it. It is Yahusha in us they hate, and He not only feels the fiery darts, but shields us from them as He stores our tears in a bottle.

Feathers In The Wind *(author unknown)*
A man who slandered went around his town repeating gossip and negative impressions about others. The evil tongue (lashon hara, slander) murders the reputation of a person. Feeling guilty, the man went to a teacher and asked what he could do to rectify the situation. He was told to take one of his feather pillows, and stand on a hill that overlooked the town, rip open the pillow, and shake the feathers out into the wind.
Next, he was told to go and collect every one of the feathers, and put them back into the pillow.
The man replied,
"I can't do that!" the man replied, *"surely the wind has taken some of them all across the town, and I will not be able to find them!"*

143

The teacher said, *"so it is with lashon hara (gossip and slander). Once you send these evil words into the community, there is no way to undo the damage, no way to reach all those who have heard it, and spread it. It is because of this that gossip and slander are like murder."*

Do not listen to gossip. Like the others, the 9th Commandment guides us to *love* our neighbor.

Do to others as you would have them do to you. The same measure we use to judge others will be used on us; forgive, and you will be forgiven.

The Scripture translations show us what the translators believed, and they were all highly influence by the Latin Vulgate in its English form, the Anglican Catholic KJV. IESV was taken from the Vulgate into the KJV in the first edition (1611), and in less than 100 years IESV began to be printed as "JESUS." The letter "J" is less than 500 years old. The Hebrew Name (Acts 4:12) is Yahusha.

The works of the devil are resisted by those who check the source (the inspired Hebrew). Once you receive the Truth, you cannot pretend the lie is the same; you *have* to expose it. The word *BIBLE* is not in any Hebrew sourced documents, but it is the name of a fertility idol worshiped at Byblos, named after the Greek idol *Byblia*. The city exported papyrus, and what we refer to as *paper* was referred to by the Greek term. The Scripture of Truth (Danial 10:21) is commonly referred to by the Greek term, *BIBLE*. Can you imagine how Yahuah feels about this?

Run! Teach All Nations! (and they are very lost) Videos tearing-down others are all over the Internet, and not limited to only political figures. For Yahuah's servants, ***"No weapon formed against you will***

prosper, and every tongue that rises against you in judgment You shall condemn. This is the heritage of the servants of Yahuah . . . "
YashaYahu 54:17

Lew White *(that's me)* is a target of malicious gossip too. An edited video with scary music made in 2012 recording me (Lew White). The video was reproduced by another person and re-edited to portray me as an idol worshiper. Their videos do not give the identity of the person or persons posting them, and they disable any ability to leave comments for viewers to ask questions. We should pray for those who would tear down the reputation of others, since this behavior grieves Yahusha. The offended person needs to talk things over privately, and certainly never tear down their reputation. Internet bullying is very common, and illegal to engage in. Yahuah will hold us accountable for every idle word we speak or write. We were all delivered by the same precious blood, and although what I was doing many years ago was taken *out of its context,* I'm sure Yahusha is allowing the gossip to spread itself to test the hearts of those who really know what is right. In the edited video, I held up a scary Halloween mask to the phone, making it seem the caller was talking to the mask. *The Halloween masks are silly folly, which is why I was holding one to talk to a customer on the phone.* The world has gone mad. I did not stock the masks, but I used the many things people do that are in the world as *teaching tools.* Some people are inhabited by demons, but those inhabited by Yahusha's Ruach do not run from the darkness, they drive them away by exposing the darkness. May Yahusha show His everlasting kindness to those who did this, and those who helped make it explode on the Internet as it has.

We consistently teach the Commandments and Name. Forgive, and you will be forgiven. By your words you will be declared upright, and by your words you will be condemned.
"No weapon formed against you will prosper, and every tongue that rises against you in judgment you shall condemn. This is the heritage of the servants of Yahuah . . . " YashaYahu 54:17

Bloom Where You're Planted, Do Not Run Away

When you turn away from the way you used to be (sinful desires, wild parties, idolatry), your friends and family who have known you for years think you are *strange* and *heap abuse* on you (1 Peter 4:3-4).
The Light does not run from the darkness, it overcomes the darkness. While you are mocked and called names by those you love, you must remain steadfast. Stay at your post. Show them His love, and bear His fruits, and He will draw them with love. They may be assuming their arrows are striking you because they think you feel what they would feel. Yahusha will guard your heart from the venom that drips from their lips. As you share words of life, Yahusha defects their words of death.
Yahusha in you is the One luring them to *obedience,* but the mind of the flesh doesn't *want* to obey, nor is it able to. Think only good thoughts toward them, showing only love with gentle encouragement. They are wrestling, and you need to be there to help, not run. Love is the greatest force in the universe, and He's alive in you. No weapon formed against you will prosper. Read YashaYahu chapters 54 and 57 to help your understanding of how Yahuah is with you, and He will assure you that you are secure in His purpose for your life.

"I am Yahuah, that is My Name" YashaYahu 42:8
At the point we realize there is only one Name (Acts 4:12), and our teachers admit they replaced that one Name (see the preface of any popular translation), we become responsible for checking everything they say. There is no transliteration for the Name in most English versions, only the replacement term they admit putting in their translations literally thousands of times.

The Roman Catholic pope issued a bull (an official dogma) in the 5th month of 2008, and that bull *forbids* the utterance of the real Hebrew Name in public worship, prayer, or song at any time. There is no letter J in Hebrew, Greek, or Latin, it's only been around less than 500 years. Jesus / Jehovah are very different from Yahusha / Yahuah. Surely these insights are tied to Danial 12, and the end of days. The only resistance to Truth is tradition. Darkness is overcome by the light; light does not run from darkness.

Yahuah is Yahusha, and He has become our Deliverer. There is no other Deliverer.

THE REAL NAME

ONE OF THESE TWO IS OF RECENT ORIGIN, AND THEREFORE A FRAUD:

JESUS OR YAHUSHA?

"YAHUSHA" means "Yah is our deliverer" in Hebrew. "JESUS" seems to convey *"hail Zeus"* in Greek, and *"the horse"* in Hebrew *(HE-SOOS)*.

Both cannot be true. Since there was no letter "J" on planet Earth until around 1530 CE, one of these two is already exposed as a hoax.
To say *"we speak English"* isn't a defense of anything, since the "only Name" given by which there is deliverance is a Hebrew Name, not an English one (Acts 4:12).
The Latin letters we use for the correct sound of the Name to call upon are called "English", but "Jesus" isn't an English word. Jesus is a Latinized form of Greek, taken from IESOUS into the Latin Vulgate as IESU. Yahuah does not change, so the Name of our Mashiak would not undergo alterations over time, so it was tampered with by an enemy. The Anti-messiah will come in the name Jesus.

Scholars know how to determine the real Name of the Mashiak of Israel, but they hesitate because *tradition* would be challenged. The evidence reveals that the person known as "Joshua" in the Scriptures has exactly the same Hebrew name as the Mashiak, because both the Mashiak and the successor of Mosheh are identical in Greek, IESOUS. The Name of the Mashiak is not Greek, but Hebrew.
The Name has a meaning in Hebrew; yet "JESUS" (or JEZUS if in Jugoslavia) is promoted by the Society of Jesus (Jesuits) to be valid based solely upon Greek, not Hebrew. This study should set the record straight, because we are going to look at the Hebrew to allow the true Name to become known.
The intermediate languages have only mutilated the original for us.

YAHUSHA & YAHUSHUA ARE BOTH CORRECT TRANSLITERATIONS

THE MASHIAK'S NAME IS FOUND **219 TIMES** IN THE TANAK.
In 216 of these, the spelling is: **yod-hay-uau-shin-ayin: YAHUSHA.**
The *son of Nun* (a leader of the tribe Ephraim / Afraim) that we find in the concordance started out with a four-lettered name, then Mosheh changed it by adding *one letter* (YOD) to the *beginning* of his name:

#1954: HAY-UAU-SHIN-AYIN (HUSHA), rendered in the KJV as HOSHEA (Dt. 32:44), and OSHEA (Num 13:16).

PAGE 1 OF 4

The Internet is flooded with all kinds of new, wild teachings that unsettle the hearts of many people.

One of the most ridiculous misunderstandings is the idea that saying *"AMEN"* is calling on a pagan deity. Truly, truly: Aman is <u>not</u> referring to the Egyptian deity Amun Ra (in Egyptian, "hidden one").

Amanah is the feminine form of **Aman**.

The words relate to agreement, affirming truth, being certain, much like the idiom "Bob's your uncle" - no problem. In the USA, we say, *"OK."*

Aman means "truly."

Beatniks would say, "I can dig it."

The Eberith word is not the name of an Egyptian deity as some teach, that is taking the word out of the context, and applying the sound of a foreign language's word to a study not related to the text. Eisegesis is not just a therapy, it's programming. Jesuit equivocation is being used all over the Internet, a specious technique also known as casuistry. It's deception, and few people know it is being employed. Learn more at this webpage: **fossilizedcustoms.com/prayer.html**

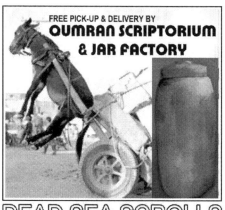

FREE PICK-UP & DELIVERY BY
OUMRAN SCRIPTORIUM & JAR FACTORY

DEAD SEA SCROLLS

Who Left The Vowels Out?

The truth is, *no one did*; the vowels are written letters.

Are there missing vowels in the Dead Sea Scrolls?

The **four vowels** of the **Name** in the Scriptures of Truth *is a word used more than any other word.* It has been treated as a forbidden word since the days of YirmeYahu (see chapter 23). Then in the 8th century CE it was more severely controlled / steered by symbols *(niqqud marks).* These were invented by men for the purpose of conforming to their phonetic standards *(rules of men). Masoretes,* a sect of Karaites, invented the twiddlydiddles / niqqud marks in the 8th century. Their name, *Masoretes, is derived from the Hebrew word masorah,* meaning *tradition.* Tehillim 102:18 tells us His Name was *written* for a future generation to <u>call</u> on His Name. Are there missing vowels in His Name, and we had to wait until the 8th-century CE for someone to invent additional symbols in order to know how to pronounce it? Mishlei 18:17 + Mishlei 28:9 x YashaYahu 9:16 = YashaYahu 8:20

HEBREW APPROACHED
BY BABBLERS:

GREEK

LATIN   ENGLISH

If we try to reason with transliterations handed-down to us through foreign languages, we miss the elephant in the room. We have to go to the source. *Eberith* (Hebrew) is the foundation to build on.

The 8th century Karaite niqqud marks are man-made and need to be ignored because vowels are *written* letters, not gnats *flying around* the words.

The prophet known as ALISHA is spelled alef-lamed-yod-shin-ayin. His name begins with an alef (A), but has been maligned to ELISHA by scholars who believe otherwise. The Dead Sea Scrolls have no such mutilating speech-guides at all.

Reasoning with only the inspired letters, we see a comparison between the spellings of ALISHA and YAHUSHA in Eberith, with the ending suffix <u>SHA</u>:

alef-lamed-yod-shin-ayin - ALISHA
(*shin-ayin* is a suffix modifying <u>ALI</u>)
yod-hay-uau-shin-ayin - YAHUSHA
(*shin-ayin* is a suffix modifying <u>YAHU</u>)

Mushah invented the spelling for YAHUSHA; see Numbers 13:16, the *first use.* He added one letter to the beginning of the name HUSHA, Y + HUSHA, forming YAHUSHA.

Before Numbers 13:16, we see the name *HUSHA* written with four letters, **hay-uau-shin-ayin** (HUSHA). At this verse, we read that Mushah began to call him Yahusha: **yod + hay-uau-shin-ayin** (YAHUSHA). You will need to see this evidence in an interlinear Hebrew-English text.

The added marks of the Masoretes (sect of Karaites founded by Anan, 767 CE) **added** vowels causing transliterations like **JOSHUA** for YAHUSHA, **JOSEPH** for YUSEF, and **ELISHA** for ALISHA.

Over the past 1200 years, this has trained readers to say "ADONAI" (ADUNI) in place of YAHUAH's Name. Yahuah disagrees with these altered terms, and tells us: ***"I am YAHUAH, that is My Name."*** YashaYahu 42:8

Have you heard teachers use Greek to excuse their avoidance of the true Hebrew Name? They may feel *"He knows who I mean,"* or feel GOD, JESUS, FATHER, WONDERFUL, or other terms are fine, even if these words did not exist until recently, and were never used to refer to Yahuah.

ATTRIBUTES & TITLES

Roles, attributes, and ***titles*** provide different ways of describing the functions our Creator has with His creation.

Examples Of *Attributes:*
James Brown, Elvis Presley, and Michael Jackson have personal names, but their *renown* describes *attributes*, what they are known by, or *called.*

Psalm 79:6 insists on a particular NAME:
"Pour out Your wrath on the nations that do not acknowledge You, on the kingdoms that refuse to call on Your Name . . . "

"GOD" won't do; there are *too many* of those.
LORD is the meaning of BEL, translated into languages such as Eberith (Aduni), Greek (Kyrios), Latin (Dominus), and English (LORD).
The translators who have done this admit it in their prefaces; check your NIV, NASB, and others.

The square-script is often referred to as *modern Hebrew, but it is Aramaic.* The Name is preserved respectfully among the foreign Aramith script from Babel on the Great Isaiah Scroll in the Shrine of the Book at Jerusalem. The founder of the Karaite sect, Anan, was arrested in 767 CE for rebellion in Babel by the ruling Caliph. The niqqud marks were later developed by his Karaite sect known as Masoretes to control the phonology as they preferred it. Since the 8th century, the Masoretic script shows us the Aramith text with dots and other marks to insert the sounds of vowels they wanted people to add. We should not malign the language, but preserve it unmolested.

"Darkness cannot drive out darkness, only the Light can do that. Hate cannot drive out hate, only Love can do that." - Martin Luther King

RACISM & BIGOTRY IN THE HUMAN RACE
All lives matter, we are all created from **one blood** - Adam. Adam was black, as were all *first people*.
Skin color is the result of genetic expression.
It is impossible for skin to become blacker over the generations, it can only *lighten*. Our outward appearance is not of any concern to Yahuah,
He created us all from one blood. To criticize what He has made is a matter He will take up with each individual bigot. When He made Miryam leprous, it was over the matter of the Cushite her brother Mushah had taken as his wife in Midian.
This was written for our example to not even think such thoughts about others who are of a different shade of skin.

When Noah was born, his father Lamech ran to Methuselah his father, for Noah's skin was *white*.
Logic dictates that Methuselah and Lamech were black. The Truth is reserved for those who seek it.

Yahusha made us all, and all mankind is the human race, and He shed His blood to purchase each one of us. Bigotry is sin, read Numbers 12.
For her words concerning the girl her brother married, Miryam was stricken with leprosy.

Our words carry life and death in them, so we should always uplift one another; never gossip or condemn, for by the standard we use to judge others, we will be judged.

WHAT IS OUR IDENTIFYING OUTWARD SIGN?
The sign is Shabath, not skin or curses.
Natsarim are a sect hated everywhere, but we count persecution as a blessing to share in the sufferings of Yahusha. The sign of the eternal Covenant between Yahuah and His people (forever) is not the curses for disobedience Yahuah promised Yisharal, but rather the sign of Shabath (resting on day 7 as He did). Hebrews 4 mentions the 7th day rest, and that it remains for the people of Alahim.
All who guard Shabath will be welcome to enjoin (by grafting in) to Him, (YashaYahu / Is. 56). The children of Abrahim are all those who obey Yahuah's Word, we are not evaluated by curses; such an argument is non-sequitur. The genealogy arguments are silly and must not be engaged in (1 Timothy 1:4). Even the Arabs are true Hebrews, in fact Yishmaal was Abrahim's first male child. They were never scattered, but remain exactly where Yahuah wanted them to be as a witness to them, and those who teach bigotry to the untaught and unstable among the nations. Natsarim are awakening to teach ALL the nations to guard everything Yahuah commanded us to obey, so they may bear the fruit of obedience.

Our Behavior Shows Obedience, Or Rebellion
"But there also came to be false prophets among the people, as also among you there shall be malicious teachers who shall secretly bring in destructive heresies and deny Aduni Who bought them, bringing swift destruction upon

154

themselves. And many shall follow their destructive ways, because of whom the way of Truth shall be evil spoken of, and in greed with fabricated words, they shall use you for gain. From of old, their judgment does not linger, and their destruction does not slumber." 2Pet. 2:1-3 BYNV

APOCRYPHAL BOOKS NOT IN BYNV

The 5 scrolls of Kanok (aka Enoch) discovered in the Dead Sea Scrolls exist, but are hidden-away. Reading them in recently-published books are only translations made by Christians re-vamped to restore better transliterations. Christian theologians have a blocked perspective of the will of Yahuah. They must feel the Hebrew documents contain damaging truth that would cause a loss of their control over doctrine. One huge problem for them is why the scrolls were preserved at Qumran in the first place: The Name of Yahuah was written on everything. *The Name of Yahuah is the most dangerous single word to their authority.* Because the Hebrew cannot be checked for context to verify the words, I have not used them in the BYNV. The same is true for all the Apocryphal books.

Apocrypha – a plural word referring to secret writings to be read only by initiates into a given Christian group. GreeK: *APO* (away) + *KRYTEIN* (secret).

From our perspective in time as Natsarim being awakened by Yahusha's Ruach, our mission is to teach all nations the Name the builders rejected, and to guard *everything* we were commanded to guard. The effects of introducing more material to delve into has caused mostly confusion and division on a variety of subjects. We know we are at the end of days. We have more information today than any generation before us.

Once we have found Truth Himself, we only need to submit to Him, not keep looking for Him.

Qoheleth 12:12-14 tells us about *books*, and what we need to know about what is *hidden* from us:

"And besides these, my son, be warned – the making of many books has no end, and much study is a wearying of the flesh.

Let us hear the conclusion of the entire matter: Fear Alahim and guard His commands, for this applies to all mankind! For Alahim shall bring every work into lawfulness, including all that is hidden, whether good or whether evil."

Qoheleth 12:12-14 BYNV

Yahusha's Greatest Commandments

The misunderstanding of Scripture is widespread across the whole Earth. Once, I heard a famous Christian pastor on a radio broadcast say "the law is a curse," but Endtime Watchmen's video explains the proper understanding (Yahusha's Greatest Commandments).

In this video, Yahusha received the "curse of the law" for us, which required the shedding of blood. Acts 20:28 is another area Christianity misunderstands. Without obedience, belief is dead. Share it:

https://youtu.be/PAZR5N5QxqA

Yahusha's Greatest Commandments (video)

Yahusha is the EXAMPLE, not the EXTERMINATOR of the Commandments. Who Do You Trust; lawless pastors, or Yahusha's Word?

Yahusha said He did not come to destroy His Commandments. He said He came to destroy the works of the devil.

DO YOU WEAR TSITSITH?

The word is based on the root, *TSITS*, meaning *blossom.* A simple purple / violet cord reminds us to *remember to obey the Torah of Yahuah.*

How to make your own to wear this reminder is so easy a child can understand and do it.

These simple reminders were worn by the most important Person in human history, and His followers imitate everything He is doing, and teaching all nations to guard everything He instructed us to guard. He calls them tsitsith, and our teachers have failed to tell us about them, so most people have never heard of them. They are trained to disobey, so why would disobedient people want to be reminded of doing anything that pleases Yahusha?

https://youtu.be/oHdJDW2afIM

UNTWISTING THE SHIBBOLETH

Where Fruit Grows on a plant

Read a detailed study at:

fossilizedcustoms.com/SHIBBOLETH_Lew_White.html

This Hebrew word was used to verify a person's identity. Websites block robots by asking you to enter what you see in a photo, and checking a box verifying you are not a robot.

We verify (see the truth of identity) a tree by examining the fruit it bears.

Shibboleth is a Hebrew word that can mean leaf, flowing growth, blossom, or branch.

It may also refer to the part of any plant that produces grain, seed, or fruit, *to identify it by.*

Giladites used this word to test the identity of men crossing the Yarden in the days of the Judges of Yisharal: **"And Gilad captured the fords of the Yarden that faced Afrayim. And it came to be**

when the fugitives from Afrayim said, 'Let me pass over,' the men of Gilad said to him, 'You are an Afrayimite!' If he said, 'No,' then they would say to him, 'Please say: *shibboleth*' - And he would say, 'sibboleth,' for he was unable to pronounce it right. Then they seized him and slew him at the fords of the Yarden. And at that time there fell 42,000 Afrayimites."
Judges 12:5-6.

We pronounce the Name differently from one another, so much so we hear vowels being treated as if they are consonants. YEHOVAH as we see it today (or JEHOVAH) is expressed with letters that sound far differently than the four vowels yod-hay-uau-hay. There is no double-U or letter J in Hebrew, and foreign lips have distorted the pure one. Alahim, Adam, and Abrahim begin with the same letter, yet often we see E used in Alahim. The letters are the rules, but men have been convinced the sounds of the letters needed their help along the way, so they made-up rules to control how they should sound in their understanding. The restoration of a pure lip is slowly turning us away from all the divisions, so let Yahusha do His marvelous refining work within each of us. What is a vowel? What is a consonant?
fossilizedcustoms.com/fourvowels.html

Are they saying Yeshua in Hebrew is translated into English as Joshua?
The point of misunderstanding on this is the difference between translating (conveying the meaning of a word into another language), and transliterating (conveying the exact sound of a word into the letters of another language's alphabet.

Are they saying the Name of Yahuah is written with four consonants, not vowels? Let's review the difference between a vowel and consonant:

CONSONANTS

Consonants are letter-sounds using the lower lip against the upper teeth *("VEE, FEE");* or both lips *("BEE & PEE");* air rushing through teeth *("SHH & SSS");* abrupt compression of air in front or back of mouth using tongue, teeth, roof of mouth *("GEE, DEE, JEE, KEE").*

VOWELS

Vowels are letter-sounds using only the breath and mouth cavity without constricting the air flow with lips, tongue, teeth, or roof of mouth. If there is any buzzing, clicking, hissing, thuds, or any abrupt stops of air heard, consonants are present. A E I O U are vowels.

Yusef Ben MatithYahu (Flavius Josephus) wrote that he saw the gold headpiece of the High Priest, and the Name was written in the Eberith script using four vowels. It was not written in Aramith, nor were there Masoretic dots added to deflect the phonology of the Name.

Let's put it another another way:

YAHUSHA is a phonetic *transliteration* for the Hebrew Name of our High Priest, Creator, and Deliverer, which the world has been taught is written JESUS (see an interlinear Hebrew-English text such as Zechariah 3:3).

The **IESV** in the Roman-Catholic Latin Vulgate was the christogram the Anglican-Catholic KJV used in the first edition. Later editions used the revised spelling JESUS. The letter J is less than 500 years old, and the ending *SUS* refers to the Greek deity

used in other words (Parnassus, Dionysus, Pegasus):
ZEUS.

He-soos means *the horse* in Hebrew.

This is why people are so easily deceived: *they don't study.* They believe every word they hear from those they choose to trust, so the Word of Yahuah does them no good. Their foundation is built on the traditions of men, not the sure foundation, Yahuah's Word (Truth). The information Age is now here, and teachings are easy to test. When beaten-down (rejected) for what they having studied and found to be true, many still value keeping their friends over walking in Truth.

Our foundation rests none of the beliefs fabricated by men. It rests on the personal relationship with our Creator, Yahuah, Who revealed His will to all mankind - those present, and not present - at Sinai. The Ten Commandments are the eternal Covenant, and animal blood (the old covenant) was placed beside the ark (Dt. 31:26, Hebrews 8:13). Yahusha offered His blood that ended the old covenant requiring animal blood. For those trusting in His perfect offering of Himself, He causes us to love His eternal Covenant, by circumcising our hearts with a love for obedience. All the lies of the dragon are dispelled when the Truth is accepted, so please let Yahusha throw out the old leaven, and allow us to enter into the coming reign without men's guile. Who's with us? We are Natsarim - Google us!

Depart From Me; I Never Knew You
The law of sin and death is no longer over us, it could redeem no one with animal blood (ceremonial law & former priesthood). The eternal Covenant is *in* the ark, not *beside* it (Dt. 31:26).

Yahuah circumcises our hearts (minds) so we love His Torah, and only then can we walk in His Torah of kindness.

The accuser has no power over us when we are sealed with Yahusha's Name if we have repented (turned away) and been forgiven (cleansed by our immersion, calling on Yahusha to forgive us). We cannot return to the pig pen after being washed. Yahuah told us many would come to Him asking to enter thinking their efforts for Him would be accepted, but He will tell them to depart, "you who work lawlessness." (anomia, Mt. 7:23)

Lawlessness is caused by those who have taught a bitterness toward obeying Him, rather than a bitterness toward disobeying Him.

He who turns His ear away from hearing the Torah, even his prayers are an abomination. (Proverbs 28:9)

When You Don't Know What To Say

Picture yourself talking with a friend who does not believe Truth, but is indoctrinated with the world order. Logic tells us that the universe around us did not create itself. After you have pledged yourself to Yahusha through water and are sealed by His Name, and redeemed by His blood for the forgiveness of your crimes, use the Word to transform the mind of your friend. Even if a person does not believe, belief comes by hearing.

"In the beginning, Alahim created the heavens and the Earth . . . "

Phrases like this will go into their ears, and begin to transform their mind by salting your conversations with the Scriptures of Truth. Romans 12 is loaded with the right way to handle ourselves in these circumstances. Let Yahusha's love call them to Him; He will use your mouth to do wonders you cannot possibly imagine. That's how He changed you and me, remember?

Our Life Begins At Our Immersion

This is why we immerse calling on the Name of Yahusha: for the forgiveness of our sins. Before going into the water, He hears us say we are willing to obey Him, and stop disobeying His Word. It's called repenting. We have to apologize, and ask Him to forgive us for our ignorance. He comes into us, sharing His Mind (viewpoint, perspective), and guides us into all Truth, but this takes study (with His help) to show we are in-line with His Word. Do we know very much at the point we call on His Name? No, we are babes, and learning to walk and talk. As we grow, He leads us out of the morass of leaven (men's teachings and ideologies), purging the dross from our hearts, and He sows the good seed there. By His calling us, He lifts us from the cesspool of humanity's idolatrous behavior. If we invest His Word in others, He will say to us, "Well done, good and trustworthy servant." If we desire only our own deliverance, and do not share the Living Water with others, we are like the Dead Sea; water goes in, but never flows out. Someone reached you; now, go and tell the nations Yahusha is coming, and His reward is with Him.

Hot Topic: Using Cannabis

Many things are *permissible*, but not *beneficial*. Plants have been and always will be the primary nutritional resource Yahuah created for all animal life on Earth. Some are used for healing, for food, for making paper, building materials, clothing, etc. The anointing oil described at Exodus / Shemoth 30:23 calls for a large percentage of **Kanna bosim**

(Latinized to *cannabis*) but the only translation showing this is the BYNV. Kanna Bosim is edible, and has been used as a medicine for thousands of years; while other plants (like poison ivy) are not. Common house plants are often found to be so toxic if eaten they can sicken or kill our pets. Yahuah created all that is seen and unseen. In the beginning He declared **"It's all good"** (a colloquial form of saying it). He wants us to happy, healthy, and helpful people. Common sense tells us to stay away from inhaling smoke, touching bare electrical wires, getting drunk, stepping on sea urchins, or not wearing a life jacket on a boat. Torah does not prohibit us from doing many things. 1 Korinthians 10:23 explains that although things may be *permissible*, they may not be *beneficial*.
Our diets, electromagnetic smog, and the polluted air and water we live with are the source of many health problems. Learn to do things that please Yahusha.

Be doers of the Word, not hearers only
Yahusha is constantly refining us, and He will finish the work He started in us.
Men's teachings placed in our minds may be widely-used but misunderstood words, false imaginations, sacraments, trinity/twinity nonsense, the incessant re-interpretation of calendars, portal connections, genetic / tribal bigotry, the shape of the planet, etc., but Yahusha can clear it all out of us, if we will only surrender to His love.
Here's the Gate that leads to eternal life, enter in if you know His Name, Yahusha. Love Him and guard His Commandments. A webpage to share:
fossilizedcustoms.com/ten.html

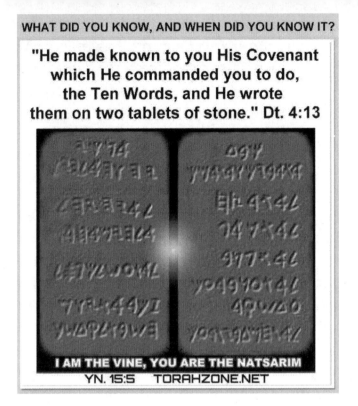

"He made known to you His Covenant
which He commanded you to do,
the Ten Words, and He wrote
them on two tablets of stone." Dt. 4:13

I AM THE VINE, YOU ARE THE NATSARIM
YN. 15:5   TORAHZONE.NET

Can A Spirit Shed Blood?

Acts 20:28 tells us we were purchased with the blood of the Ruach ha Qodesh, and yet a Spirit would have to inhabit a body in order to shed His own blood. The One we have to do with had to become omnipresent (in space), omniscient (all knowing), and omnitemporal (existing in all time, or rather outside time). These skills are required for Yahusha to be all-in-all, and be *"Mashiak in you"* as the *Paraklita* (Helper, Comforter) that we <u>know</u> He truly is.

The goal we all share is love for Yahuah and one another, and those who obey Him belong to Him. Our commission is to teach the Name and Word, and beyond that our personal relationship with Him can go further, but we should not cause our understanding of Who He is to become divisive.

I'm unworthy to be His servant, but still, I seek to do everything I can to serve Him. He makes us worthy by cleaning us on the inside. He's omnipresent. No created being can be in two places at once, ride two horses going in two different directions, or for that matter, heal as Yahusha can.

He will call us out of our graves one day, if He tarries to help more to come in before our bodies die, because He is our Shepherd.

If you have any interest in seeing the Scriptures He opened my heart to understand which revealed more about Who He is, have a look with this link.

If after reading this page I seem to be twisting things out of context, we can agree to disagree.

fossilizedcustoms.com/omnipresence.html

Natsarim love Yahusha and teach others to obey (walk) _as_ He obeyed (walked). Yahusha can hear us if we pray to Him, because we obey His Commandments and do the things that are pleasing to Him. For those who turn their ears away from hearing His Torah, their prayers are an abomination to Him; Proverbs 28:9.

Yahuah's Everlasting Kindness

The scattering of the tribes across the time zones of Earth, the interpretation of the confused languages, and even the artificial convention of an International Date Line are certainly influences that only Yahusha can overcome. The Jewish calendars often print Shabuoth on the wrong date because their convention insists that First-Fruits is always on Abib 16. As each of us tests all these things with Scripture, and Yahusha removes the inherited errors of Babel from His bride, the main goal is love, enduring, and encouraging the bride to look to Yahusha without distractions. Yahusha's love is pulling us through an enormous junkyard of men's teachings that are cross-pollinated with all sorts of pagan associations, but on the day He appears, we will all be made ready by Him, and we will feel only His irresistible loving kindness, and everlasting forgiveness.

Yahusha is our Passover, the Lamb of Alahim.
He is the Redeemer from beginning to end in the Scriptures of Truth. His indwelling destroys the works of the devil, not His Commandments.
Those who know Him guard and teach them.
The remembrance of His death on the 14th between the evenings (nearing sunset prior to the 15th) is observed by all immersed followers of His teachings. The beginning of the 14th of the first month also holds great meaning to His last Natsarim alive today. Nearing sunset on the 13th, we observe the example of the remembrance supper He had with His followers as we read His final instructions to the first Natsarim before His death. From the beginning to the end of the 14th, we meditate on the time He took the bread and the cup of wine, prayed in the garden, was arrested and mistreated all night and the following day. After Yahusha finished His last meal with His first Natsarim, He had already begun to die. As He prayed fervently in the garden, He was shedding blood in His sweat. Every drop that He spilled counts, and every moment leading up to His final breath the next afternoon is part of the remembrance each of us cherish dearly. Yahusha's last Natsarim are here on the Earth again, appealing to all mankind: be restored to favor.

Christianese Has Distorted The Besorah
Consider what you have not heard.

Those who obey receive the Spirit of Yahusha (Acts 5:32), and He helps us to understand, and do the things that are pleasing to Him by the power of His Spirit living in us.

Demons believe, but they do not obey. Repenting means to turn from sin, and trust in the perfect offering of Yahusha's blood that cleanses us from our past sins, and the penalty of death required for those sins.

We pledge ourselves to Him by the act of immersion, calling on the one Name (Yahusha, Acts 4:12) for the forgiveness of our crimes against His eternal Covenant. If we claim we know Him, and do not guard His Commandments, we lie, and the Truth (His Word) is not in us (1 Yn. 3:4). The "old" covenant was written a scroll and placed beside the ark, and that old priesthood and the prescribed animal blood is no longer functional (See Dt. 31:26, Hebrews 6:13). Animal blood is imperfect to redeem anyone. The renewed Covenant is cut, and our minds are circumcised by our belief in Yahusha's blood which He has given for us.

He has redeemed us completely by His own blood, the one perfect offering as our High Priest. The Ruach ha Qodesh gave Himself to purchase us with His own blood (Acts 20:28).

YAHUSHA DELIVER ME!

Who Were You Taught To Call On For Deliverance?

3000 People Were Immersed After Hearing These Words (Acts 2:38):

"Repent and be immersed, every one of you, in the Name of Yahusha Mashiak for the forgiveness of yours sins, and you will receive the gift of the Ruach ha Qodesh."

You only need Yahusha and a pool of water to be immersed, He is the One you have to call on for **deliverance**, and then you will see others as He sees them. Where His Ruach dwells, love dwells. If you love Yahusha, obey Him, and keep your eyes fixed on Him, or you'll sink. May the workers in His harvest increase the moment you come up from the waters!

Zodiac Madness

The constellations / zoo imagined to be in the *host of heaven* worshiped by the nations are what Yahuah refers to in the 2nd Commandment, and evokes a very high degree of jealous rage in Him to see His children misled by them, or to pay any attention to them. They are not real, only imagined.

The worship of the *host of heaven* is the old astrology system from Babel, and Stephen warned the assembly about it at Acts 7:42. YirmeYahu (Jer.) 10:2 and Ayub (Job) 31:27 show us Yahuah's perspective on the subject. Even the elect may be enticed into thinking these practices from Babel are indicators of Yahusha's return. Flee from these concepts, and warn others: anathema! maranathah! (forbidden! Master comes!)

fossilizedcustoms.com/zodiac.html

Do Not Learn The Way Of The Heathen

As we perform a careful study of the festivals of Yahuah, Enoch is not mentioned in them. They represent the outline (shadow) of Yahuah's redemption plan for all who seek and obey Him.

The confusion among teachers on the calendar is an ever-expanding alternate universe where crowds are following cross-pollinated teachings based on Kabbalah, Jewish mysticism, and a rich blend of Babel's zoo animals.

Images in the skies, or a *heavenly scroll*, are believed to contain messages about mankind's redemption plan, and Yahusha's return to reign. These things are forbidden by the second Commandment. YirmeYahu 10 explicitly tells us not to learn the things the nations fear. The worship of the *host of heaven* was mentioned by Stephen before they took him out and stoned him to death for uttering the Name of Yahuah. (Acts 7)

The word *imagination* is based on the word image. Teachers *imagine*, and those who listen to them are *confused*. Look at YashaYahu 44:25, and surrounding verses. The practice of counting the omer is not found in Scripture, but calculating the 7 weeks between First-Fruits and Shabuoth is easy to understand by reading Uyiqara 23 & Debarim 16. Yahuah's appointed times are easy when read from His Word, not explained by teachers. They are Yahuah's redemption plan for all mankind.

From First-Fruits during Matsah to the 50th day after is the calculation for Shabuoth. The unfulfilled appointed times occur in the 7th month, ushering-in the reign of Yahusha.

Is "Count" A Verb Or Noun?

Someone recently asked about the "counting of the omer" tradition, and wondered about the traditional word Pentecost. The Hebrew is the true source, but the Greek and Latin influences distort quite a bit. Pentecost means "count fifty" in Greek, and is an invented word through translation referring to Shabuoth (weeks). The Greek word Pentecost is a compound word having two components. Peninta is the Greek word for fifty. Komitos is the medieval Greek for "count," from KOMIS. The Latinized form of Komitos produces the cost component we've inherited. The Hebrew Roots of our belief, and most words, steer us away from the path of truth, but with careful study we can restore a better understanding.

The Hebrew Word "Count"

SEPARTIM (H5608) is a verb meaning count, number, enumerate, calculate, or reckon, and it's used in verses 15 & 16 of Uyiqara (Lev.) 23. In verse 15 we calculate SHEBA SHABATHUTH (7 Sabbaths) from the Wave Sheaf offering; in verse 16 the word is used again in reference to the sum of fifty days by including the day following the 7th Shabath. This makes it certain that the date of Shabuoth is always on a first day of a week, and reflects the pattern of the Shemitah (7th year rest for the land) and the fiftieth year when property ownership is restored in the year of Yobel (Jubilee).

To the Torah and to the Witness!

Riots in many cities after dark are going on recently. Marauding bands of violent inciters travel to these places to bring chaos among otherwise peaceful protesters. The spiritual side of these events is obviously the true source of the evil being unleashed.

Summer heat, the economic collapse from coronavirus-induced job losses, and the media constantly reporting on unlawful actions by a small number of the law enforcement community provide conditions for a perfect storm, even in otherwise peaceful cities where nothing is wrong. Evil spirits are real, and enter into anyone's house (mind) not inhabited by the Spirit of Yahusha. The lawless is increasing because the pastors teach a bitterness toward obedience, making the way of Truth seem to be evil (2 Peter 2:2). School teachers are not allowed to teach the Ten Commandments of kindness to the children. The end of days is at hand, therefore be watchful and take every opportunity to teach the Name of Yahuah and His Word to all you possibly can. Read about the solution from Malachi 4:1-6, and ask pastors why they have failed to teach this solution.

False Worship Abounds
Indoor altars, images, monstrances, bowing, lighting candles like Hindus with prayers associated with them, sacraments, Bel towers, cruxes, wreaths, tree decorating, hand gestures, prayers to dead (necromancy), bead-praying, holy water, zodiacs, and so many other false teachings will be the fuel for the fire coming on the Earth. Yahusha is the only - the one Name - we must call on for the forgiveness of our crimes against Him, and He is the Creator and Possessor of Shamayim and Arets. The builders rejected the Stone, His Name, and every false translation proves this.
Read the Preface of your translation. His Name is not LORD or any other device; He says, "I am Yahuah; that is My Name!" (YashaYahu 42:8)

Is Jesus The Antichrist? (Another Yahusha)
https://youtu.be/CKC47PQXV_4
(youtube video with this author)
The Truth sounds ridiculous at first, yet it will be shown to be self-evident after careful study.

There is only one Name given under heaven among men by which we must be delivered (Acts 4:12). Men invented the name JESUS, but the true Mashiak came to destroy the works of the devil, not Yahuah's Commandments. The whole world is deceived. Yahusha is the one Name by which we are Delivered, and it means *"I am your Deliverer."*
What does Jesus mean?
Natsarim guard the Name and the Word.
Yeh-Zus is the Antichrist, the lawless one coming in an impostor's name.

The pastors of Christianity don't understand what the renewed Covenant is. When they explain what they think it is, we are told to stay away from the Ten Commandments, or else we are will think we are earning our deliverance! Yahusha helps us see what is good, and as the Paraklita (Helper) gives us the strength to obey them, and we see how the "way of Truth" has been maligned (2 Peter 2:2). The "old" Covenant was not about redemption, but rather animal blood temporarily covered crimes through the old priesthood offering it year by year for the unintentional crimes. This *old covenant* was written on a scroll (Dt. 31:26), and place *beside* the ark. The text explaining the *change* of this law of sin and death, and the change in the priesthood, is explained at Hebrews 8:13. Yahusha's blood redeemed all who turn back to obedience, accepting His perfect offering

of Himself. Our list of crimes is wiped clean: Cheirographon - *What is it?*
This study will equip you with information you never realized you needed. Download the tract by this title at **www.torahzone.net** – it's free.

You will discover secrets that seminary-trained teachers never told you because they use mind-scrubbing therapies on crowds, not raw Truth.
In the BYNV, Danial 8:12-13 reads:
"And because of transgression, an army was given over to the horn to oppose that which is continual. And it threw the Truth down to the ground, and it acted and prospered. Then I heard a certain qodesh one speaking. And another qodesh one said to that certain one who was speaking, "Till when is the vision, concerning that which is continual, and the transgression that lays waste, to make both the qodesh place and the host to be trampled under foot?""

Gabrial describes the *duration of desolation*, and the *time of the end*. The word TAMID (H8548) is found in verses 11 and 13. As I've translated it in the BYNV, the word **continual** is a better understanding for us than *sacrifices* or *daily*.
The same word can mean different things depending on what it is referring to.
The *regular operation* of the qodesh place is being referred to, and now it is being trampled (desolated) underfoot by the invaders. Continual control over the place where Yahuah placed His Name was lost, and now the image of the **destroyer** (the dome, or shivalingam) has been built in the place where it should not be.

More about the Abomination of Desolation, which is already "set up" (built):
fossilizedcustoms.com/abomination.html

I Was Educated By The Jesuit-Illuminati
Yes; I was educated by Loyola's Societas IESV from a young age, yet I perceived something behind it all that caused me to doubt the veracity of the authority the "order" claimed to have. The order goes by many names, and there is a video I recommend you watch to expose more of their aims to control the world. They are highly-skilled infiltrators, but I assure you I was never a follower of their programming. Here's a link to a video about the World Order from the perspective of one who was educated by the Jesuit-Illuminati: **https://youtu.be/20QZB4-f0Ic**

Test What You Are Taught
Often, it is by questioning teachings we come to a knowledge of the Truth. *When was the last time you heard a pastor give a sermon on 1 Yn. 2:3-7?*

"And by this we know that we know Him, if we guard His commands. The one who says, "I know Him," and does not guard His commands, is a liar, and the truth is not in him. But whoever guards His Word, truly the love of Yahuah has been perfected in him. By this we know that we are in Him. The one who says he lives in Him ought himself also to walk even as He walked. Beloved, I write no original unfamiliar command to you, but an old command which you have had from the beginning. The old command is the Word which you heard from the beginning."

Can a person obey the Ten Commandments and still use foreign names for Yahuah?

Most likely if a person began to live by them his assembly would ask him not to come back among them. Christians are taught not to obey them, yet Yahusha lived by them and taught them. He is also the Helper Who guides us in them. Assemblies are taught to guard the traditions of their pastors. Yahusha's followers were given their name by Yahusha Himself:

"I am the Vine; you are the Natsarim."
ANI HA GAFEN; ATAH HA NATSARIM

Paul was accused of being a ringleader of the Natsarim at Acts 24:5. He also claimed that he followed the Torah, and in fact agreed with the Torah as a way of life, not his former life, the traditions of the fathers. He no longer walked as an anti-missionary, a Natsarim-slayer. The translators removed the Name of Yahuah from the texts, and they admit doing so in their Prefaces. The word JESUS did not exist until the 17th century, and is a replacement name the world has accepted. Questions serve a good purpose, and I hope everyone keeps asking them.

Whom Do You Seek?

The hearts of Yahusha's followers are the ARK containing the Ten Words He made us love. His Name seals us at our immersion as His property. For those looking for His Temple, look no further; we are His Dwelling Place. Yahusha said, "I am the Vine; you are the Natsarim."

Unless Yahuah builds the house, the builders labor in vain (Ps. 127:1). Yahusha's Name seals us for the day of the redemption of our bodies, His living stones. The *Spirit* and the *bride* says, *"come."*

More Resources

Margaret St. Peter talks about how she was inspired to write her first book in a video interview with Phyllis and Lew White.

She was searching diligently for the Truth, and did not give up. What she found was so compelling and real, she had to tell everyone that she could, and started to plan a website. It turned into the book: ***4 Steps Through The Narrow Gate - This Is The Way, Walk In It.***

Margaret hopes this book will help people find the Truth. **https://youtu.be/2BgGOXLrGC0**

You can download the eBook in seconds.
It's also available as a printed book.

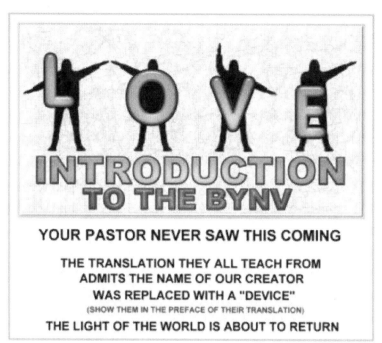

YOUR PASTOR NEVER SAW THIS COMING

THE TRANSLATION THEY ALL TEACH FROM
ADMITS THE NAME OF OUR CREATOR
WAS REPLACED WITH A "DEVICE"
(SHOW THEM IN THE PREFACE OF THEIR TRANSLATION)
THE LIGHT OF THE WORLD IS ABOUT TO RETURN

Love is a book containing the Introduction and
Glossary found in the BYNV translation.

Last Natsarim are now here to bring the
final warning to all inhabitants of the Earth.
The reign of Yahusha is near.

NO CANDY HERE SIGN PDF 24" x 24"

Show the lost what Halloween looks like from Yahusha's perspective.

Use the PDF for making posters, yard-signs, sharing in email blasts, and whatever you like. Christmas, Easter, Halloween, Valentine's Day, birthday cakes, Sun-day, and other practices are highly thought of among men, but abominations in the sight of Yahuah (Luke 16:14-15). People learned these as children, and most never break the spell of their stronghold.

This PDF is also available on a CD-R with many other items to help awaken the lost:

AMBASSADISC - A DIGITAL LIBRARY

A useful and powerful Natsarim resource is the AMBASSADISC, a CD-R with over 100 tracts, cards, and signs for your use. All are PDF to help prevent font issues, and sized for immediate printing. Ambassadisc is a resource you can use right away with unbound possibilities.

Most of the tracts are printable on a single sheet of paper and may be distributed in a variety of ways. Use it as an outreach for prison ministries, group studies, mailings, email attachments, and more. Fill the world with the Truth, and not the pastors' traditions. Link to order the Ambassadisc: **https://www.torahzone.net/AMBASSADISC.html**

Instructions for printing tracts:
Tracts are formatted for landscape, double-sided, do not shrink, black ink on white paper.
For cards and signs, follow uploading instructions (we recommend Vistaprint).

Each tract has 4 pages, and a few front pages are shown below; if this is the eBook, expand each photo.
Download selected tracts FREE: torahzone.net.
After registering, add titles to your cart, and an email will be sent to you with a link for you to download your selections.

FALL OF BABEL
AT THE TIME OF THE END

The world has been led to expect a far different outcome than will actually be experienced. The Scripture of Truth describes a very rebellious and disobedient population in the last days, and those thinking they will be justified for believing, and not *obeying*, will be in for the shock of their lives. *Get ready for the ride of your life.*

A little flock of Yahusha's ambassadors are leading many to His *Name*, to obey His *Commandments*, calling them to turn from *idolatry*, and be delivered. This is the order given by Him to the first Natsarim (Mt. 28:20), and now He is awakening the last Natsarim through the pressures (distress) in these last days. Like the plagues He sent on the disobedient Egyptians, the whole world will watch the fulfillment of 2 Kronicles 7:13-15, Dan. 12, YashaYahu / Is. 24, and Mt. 24:11-13.

Get out of the circus, reapers are coming!

A Covenant With Death

Pastors have removed The Name from their translations, and trained their assemblies to be disobedient and lawless, validation that they have made a covenant with death. All of them are blind to the idolatry, and ignore Yahuah's instructions.

"Therefore hear the Word of Yahuah, you men of scorn, who rule this people who are in Yerushalim, because you have said, 'We have made a covenant with death, and with the grave we have effected a vision. When the overflowing scourge passes through, it does not come to us,

for we have made lying our refuge, and under falsehood we have hidden ourselves.' Therefore thus said Aduni Yahuah, 'See, I am laying in Tsiun a Stone for a foundation, a tried Stone, a precious corner-stone, a settled foundation. He who trusts shall not hasten away. And I shall make lawfulness the measuring line, and obedience the plummet. And the hail shall sweep away the refuge of lies, and the mayim overflow the hiding place. And your covenant with death shall be annulled, and your vision with the grave not stand.

PAGE 1 OF 4   GET TRACT FREE AT TORAHZONE.NET

THE REAL NAME

		6,823	216	2	1
		YAHUAH	YAHUSHA	YAHUSHUA	Y'SHUA
HEBREW		ayal	oywal		oywl
ARAMAIC		ה‎ו‎ה‎י‎	ע‎ש‎ו‎ה‎י‎	ע‎ו‎ש‎ו‎ה‎י‎	ע‎ש‎י‎
GREEK		IAOUE	IHSOUS		
LATIN		IEHOUAH	IESU		

AT HEBREWS 4 AND ACTS 7 THE SAME GREEK LETTERING IS USED FOR "JOSHUA" AND "JESUS" - IHSOUS
THIS IS CONFIRMATION BOTH WERE CALLED YAHUSHA IN HEBREW
TORAH INSTITUTE

ONE OF THESE TWO IS OF RECENT ORIGIN, AND THEREFORE A FRAUD:

JESUS OR YAHUSHA?

"YAHUSHA" means "Yah is our deliverer" in Hebrew. "JESUS" seems to convey "hail Zeus" in Greek, and "the horse" in Hebrew (HE-SOOS).

Both cannot be true. Since there was no letter "J" on planet Earth until around 1530 CE, one of these two is already exposed as a hoax. To say "we speak English" isn't a defense of anything, since the "only Name" given by which there is deliverance is a Hebrew Name, not an English one (Acts 4:12). The Latin letters we use for the correct sound of the Name to call upon are called "English", but 'Jesus' isn't an English word. Jesus is a Latinized form of Greek, taken from IESOUS into the Latin Vulgate as IESU. Yahuah does not change, so the Name of our Mashiak would not undergo alterations over time, so it was tampered with by an enemy. The Anti-messiah will come in the name Jesus.

Scholars know how to determine the real Name of the Mashiak of Israel, but they hesitate because tradition would be challenged. The evidence reveals that the person known as "Joshua" in the Scriptures has exactly the same Hebrew name as the Mashiak, because both the Mashiak and the successor of Mosheh are identical in Greek, IESOUS. The Name of the Mashiak is not Greek, but Hebrew. The Name has a meaning in Hebrew; yet "JESUS" (or JEZUS if in Jugoslavia) is promoted by the Society of Jesus (Jesuits) to be valid based solely upon Greek, not Hebrew. This study should set the record straight, because we are going to look at the Hebrew to allow the true Name to become known. The intermediate languages have only mutilated the original for us.

YAHUSHA & YAHUSHUA ARE BOTH CORRECT TRANSLITERATIONS

THE MASHIAK'S NAME IS FOUND 216 TIMES IN THE TANAK.

In 216 of these, the spelling is: yod-hay-uau-shin-ayin: YAHUSHA. The son of Nun (a leader of the tribe Ephraim / Afraim) that we find in the concordance started out with a four-lettered name, then Mosheh changed it by adding one letter (YOD) to the beginning of his name:

#1954: HAY-UAU-SHIN-AYIN (HUSHA), rendered in the KJV as HOSHEA (Dt. 32:44), and OSHEA (Num 13:16).

PAGE 1 OF 4

TURNED ASIDE TO MYTHS

WHAT ARE THEY, WHO'S DOING IT, AND WHAT COULD POSSIBLY GO WRONG?

DON'T SHIVA ME BRO!
I'M YOUR HUCKLE-FAIRY!

WHY DOES CHRISTIANITY LOOK LIKE SUN WORSHIP?

Sound doctrines are all now replaced by traditions of men. Futility, lies, and myths have filled the earth with customs people embrace as familiar, and the Truth has become thought of as evil. Paul wrote of these things to Timothy: *"Proclaim the Word! Be urgent in season, out of season. Correct, warn, appeal, with all patience and teaching. For there shall be a time when they shall not bear sound teaching, but according to their own desires, they shall heap up for themselves teachers tickling the ear, and they*

shall indeed turn their ears away from the Truth, and be turned aside to myths." 2Timothy 4:2-4
A myth is a widely-held belief, among these are sacraments, holy water, transubstantiation, Sun-day, Trinities, celibacy, image worship, popes, nuns, monks, steeples, obelisks, wreaths, lent, chants, special days, prayers to the dead, indulgences, pilgrimages, stigmatas, Easter egg hunts, Dec. 24th Solstice birth, Santa, elves, trees in homes, monstrances, bells, and all forms of fertility patterns of Babel.

TEACHING AS TEACHINGS THE COMMANDS OF MEN

Luke reports for us in Acts about many events spanning about 32 years after the death and resurrection of Yahusha. He describes many of the challenges faced by his fellow traveler and convert we know as Paul. Paul was formerly known as Shaul, who had been given authority by the Sanhedrin to arrest the Natsarim (branches) in the assemblies found to be uttering Yahuah's Name,

which they called blasphemy. Shaul was confronted by Yahusha in Person on his way to Damascus. Paul was gifted with skills and mentored by Gamaliel, the grandson of the noble Torah teacher Hillel. Paul was able to speak to anyone who would listen, and was not intimidated in the least by any lawyers, judges, sophists, governors or kings.

PAGE 1 OF 4 - GET ENTIRE TRACT: TORAHZONE.NET

TETRAGRAMMATON
THIS IS MY NAME FOREVER

EXCERPT FROM THE BOOK, TETRAGRAMMATON
TETRAGRAMMATON
THE MOST ENDURING NAME IN THE UNIVERSE

Transliterating The Four Vowels

A Name Hidden For Ages

Transliteration uses letters to make a word sound the same using foreign scripts. Vowels are sounded using only the mouth cavity and breath. What is a vowel, and how do they differ from consonants?
A vowel is a letter sounded without the lips, lower lip with upper teeth, closed teeth, hissing, tongue on the roof of the mouth, or guttural stop in the throat. The shape of the mouth

cavity is used. If we hear buzzing, hissing, clicking, or the tongue stops the air as in the word giggle, you are making the sound of a consonant.
The Name of our Creator is written in four vowels: yod-hay-uau-hay, sounded as YAHUAH, not YEHOVAH. "VEE" is not a letter in the Tetragrammaton. The Latin letter V sounded as our U. VENUS (a false deity) was pronounced UENUS. The Greek letters IAOUE

Some sample content of tracts you can download free (first pages shown here).
Or get them all quickly; there are over 100 tracts on the AMBASSADISC digital library.
Each tract is 4 pages, and formatted to print double-sided on a single sheet of paper.

IDOLATRY
MANKIND'S MOST PROMINENT ACTIVITY

MANKIND'S DEFINITION
Extreme admiration, love, or reverence of something or someone; worship of a physical object or person.
YAHUAH'S DEFINITION
Setting one's thoughts or actions on anything above Yahuah. He gives an example for us from His prophets, such as YashaYahu (Isaiah) 44:16.
IDOL EXAMPLES: politicians / rulers; movie or music idols, statues, pillars, toasting with drinks; prayers to any entities other than Yahuah, spirits, dead people (necromancy, beads). Expressions we hear used all the time in conversations, and the things we run out to buy and decorate with show how invested we are in all the witchcraft, and hardly ever associate them with idolatry; rosaries, steeples horseshoes and rabbits' feet for good luck - bringing trees into our homes to celebrate a birthday, Black F-day, "let's keep our fingers crossed," horoscopes, palmistry, fortune cookies, baking cakes for

birthdays, cone hats, toasting, blowing-out candles, wishes, eggs in baskets and rabbits in the spring, sunrise services, giving candy to costumed children on the day of the dead, Valentine's Day gifts, cards, hearts, and using decorations that remind everyone that we encourage the idolatry that drives the world's economy. *the golden cup of Babel has caused madness!*

DRIVING THE WORLD ECONOMY

Every merchant prospers from the fertility celebrations that hardly anyone perceives because they are all hypnotized from a lifetime of exposure to the traditions handed-down from our fathers to children. **Idolatry** is exactly what Yahusha referred to as *stumbling blocks* at Mt. 18:3-8. Idolatry is taught to *children*, and passes into each new generation through family bonding.

Yahuah is sending the plagues now, but most people remain clueless to why Revelation 9:20
"And the rest of mankind, who were not killed by these plagues, did not repent of the works of their hands, that they should not worship the demons, and idols of gold, and of silver, and of brass, and of stone, and of wood, which are neither able to see, nor to hear, nor to walk. Merchants exploit the wormwood that causes the masses to stay drunk on the idolatrous fertility traditions.

LAST NATSARIM
AMBASSADORS OF THE REIGN OF YAHUSHA

NATSARIM ARE VERY REAL
We were prophesied to appear by YirmeYahu 31:6, and Revelation 12:17 explains we are the first-fruits, enraging the dragon because we obey the Testimony of Yahusha. Christianity was born at Alexandria, Egypt, and reinforced by the authority of Rome beginning at Nicaea in 325 CE. The Natsarim were based at Antioch just prior to the destruction of the Temple, and had to hide themselves from the Magisterium for over 1000 years. We were forced to dwell in the hills and valleys, and called *Passagians*, Albigensians, Waldenses, and Huguenots. We are proclaiming the Name of Yahusha around the world as His envoys. A Catholic website mentioned this author's name, and I attempted to answer their questions about the Natsarim, but was blocked permanently. I saved the discourse as had up to that point, and now share it with you.

Has Anyone Heard Of The Cult Of The Natsarim?

CATHOLIC FORUM TOPIC: NATSARIM
Because my name, Lew White, came up on a Catholic forum, I registered to respond to several questions being asked about what they referred to as *"the cult of the Natsarim."* This is the entire, but brief, interaction I had with the Jesuits. You will find their final response very interesting.

Jesuit question to the forums:
Has anyone heard of the cult of the Natsarim? What are its core beliefs and how does it relate to Jewish and Christian religion?

My reply: The term Natsarim is used to describe the original followers of Yahusha of Natsarith at Acts 24:5.

CHRISTIANS ARE IN TROUBLE
PASTORS ARE LEARNING ABOUT THEIR TRADITIONS

"Christians Are In Trouble"
- says a resigned pastor . .
Christian pastors are beginning to learn there is something very wrong with their traditions. They perceive a circular pattern in their festivals, then discover the outward crust is only masking the pagan origins of their practices.

READ THE GLOBAL CURSE AT MAL. 4
CANCEL YOUR COVENANT WITH DEATH
BE RESTORED TO FAVOR

the worship of the host of heaven, Christmas, New Year, Valentines, Easter, Mother & Father Days, and Halloween are celebrated world-wide, and all the merchants promote each of these **fertility** festivals many weeks ahead to exploit the sleeping hypnotized crowds. Their pastors sit and watch, never blowing the shofar to warn anyone. Their doctrines are built on sand, not based on the Scripture of Truth, so their witness is without a firm foundation. **If you begin to do what is written in the Word, they ask you NOT TO ATTEND their assembly.**
Christian pastors are resigning all around the world in order to serve Yahusha, not their denomination's orders. They are renouncing their 'ordination' to teach lies. One pastor actually stated that

Christians are in trouble:
"We want to come into more understanding about certain doctrines and desire to be baptized in the Name of our Savior Yahusha to the [esteem] of Yahuah Myself in Christianity was a preacher with general license. My wife and I resigned from this religion on 12-11-18. On 14 December we came shockingly into the understanding that Christianity is false and that Christians are in trouble."
Daniel 12, Mt. 24, and Malaki 4 are being recognized by those hearing the call of Yahusha. Those who know Him abide in His Word, and they know the Truth. All else is witchcraft (rebellion).

BEWARE THE BLOB
DESCRIBING THE LAST DAYS - YIRMEYAHU 16:19

ITS PURPOSE IS TO MAKE MORE OF ITSELF

"Beware the leaven of the Pharisees"

The 1958 movie, The Blob, could be a metaphor for how religion takes on a life of its own, and everyone is absorbed into it.
The purpose of its existence is to make more of itself.
YirmeYahu 16:19 shows we've inherited lies through traditions handed-down to us. Religion is tradition, and it develops over time as it corrupts itself by men guided by their minds of flesh.
Yahusha's yoke is light, without ritual, liturgy, or hierarchy.
We have direct access to His love. He created each of us to be His companions, and His Torah is instruction for us how to love Him, and how to love our neighbor. Torah points to the ideal relationship for bearing the perfect fruit of good behavior.
Religious tradition is like the Blob blindly performing its purpose of absorbing, growing, and competing for dominance.
The Covenant is the marriage we celebrate at the marriage supper, and the Blob serves the purpose of annihilating it.
Our choice is between the **Covenant** (life), and the **Blob** (death).
RABBINICAL JUDAISM
Question: What is the leaven, or yeast of the Pharisees?
Answer: Rabbinic Judaism, the *traditions of the fathers*.

Some sample content of tracts you can download free (first pages shown here).
Or get them all quickly; there are over 100 tracts on the AMBASSADISC digital library.
Each tract is 4 pages, and formatted to print double-sided on a single sheet of paper.

AWAKENING THE WATCHMEN

"For the people shall dwell in Tsiun at Yerushalim, you shall weep no more. He shall show much favor to you at the sound of your cry; when He hears, He shall answer you. Though Yahuah gave you bread of adversity and water of affliction, your Teacher shall no longer be hidden. But your eyes shall see your Teacher, and your ears hear a word behind you, saying, 'This is the Way, walk in it,' whenever you turn to the right, or whenever you turn to the left. And you shall defile the covering of your graven images of silver, and the plating of your moulded images of gold. You shall throw them away as a menstrual cloth and say to them, 'Be gone!'" - YashaYahu 30:19-22 BYNV

This calling-out from the pigsty is happening as Yahusha's Ruach ha Qodesh pours into men and women. He is calling them away from the circuses, bells, steeples, candles, Sun-day meetings, and all the rest of the traditions of men. Challenge yourself to listen.

A PERSONAL TESTIMONY

This is how Yahusha turned me around: reading His Word of Truth. Pastors insist we read it, but never to obey what it says. They know the Truth is powerful, but like *wizards*, they want to be the *controllers of that power*. They were so repulsed when they heard me tell them I love obeying and teaching others to obey, they went to work destroying my reputation, warning others to avoid me. In the late 1990's, a conference of Texan pastors was called to discuss what might be done about my book, *Fossilized Customs*. It was causing them a great deal of trouble. It only takes one watchmen to cause 1000 to **flee**. It was not me at all, but Yahusha inside one of His Natsarim they were afraid of. When Truth sets us free from Nimrod's minions, Yahusha makes us ambassadors of His reign. Through us, He calls every person to repent because His reign is about to appear. The flesh does not, nor can it obey Yahuah's Turah without the calling, intervention, guidance, and assistance of Yahusha's Ruach ha Qodesh. Without realizing it, religious teachers are working against Yahusha by denying His Name, disobeying His Commandments,

---

ABOMINATION OF DESOLATION
IMAGE OF THE DESTROYER OF CIVILIZATION

The Hebrew concept of SHIQUTS is an image, translated **abomination**. The messenger Gabriel was sent to Danial about events in the future. An apocalyptic message concerning an **abomination of desolation** was referred to. As we search for this **destroyer of civilization**, we easily find what cannot be mistaken by anyone aware of history, or even the daily news. It will endure to the end.

SHIVA DOME
IMAGE OF DESTROYER
ABOMINATION OF DESOLATION
IN THE QODESH PLACE

READER WILL UNDERSTAND – MT 24:15

Danial 12:11 describes the setting-up of an abomination, a common Hebrew interpretation for an idol, or **form**. Mt. 24:15 Refers to this text. Yahusha told us **the reader** would understand in the end times. The idolatrous **form** associated with **desolation** is the Shiva dome, and it is set up (built) in a **qodesh place**: the Temple Mount. The **destroyer** in the Hindu trinity is **Shiva**, whose **image** is primarily the **crescent** symbol, associated with a **star**. The star represents his wife Shakti (avatar of Parvati). The Shrines of Shiva the **destroyer** typically involve a **dome-shaped feature** (Shiva's phallus), the practice of circumambulation (walking around), a **shivalingam**, and a mat (a sacred space on which to bow to the idol). These Hindu features are expressed at the Shiva shrine at Mecca, and imitated at all other Muslim shrines around the world. As Christianity absorbed certain practices via Roman Sun worship, Islam reflects a Hindu version of the ancient Nimrod culture.

DOMED ARCHITECTURE

The Masonic connection to Shiva worship involves symbols such as the **crescent and star**, as well as the **dome designs** seen in the architecture of many religious and governmental buildings all over the Earth. The Masons worship a **great architect**, the original builder of the tower at Babel, Nimrod. If we combine all these elements, the perfect candidate for the **abomination of desolation** (destroyer) is the Shiva shrine built on the Temple Mount by Muslims.

ISLAM: DESTROYER OF CIVILIZATION

John Wesley on Islam:

"Ever since the religion of Islam appeared in the world, the espousers of it ... have been as wolves and tigers to all other nations, rending and tearing all that fell into their merciless paws; and grinding them with their iron teeth; that numberless cities are razed from the foundation, and only their name remaining; that many countries, which were once as the garden of God,

---

DOERS OF THE WORD
NOT HEARERS ONLY, DECEIVING YOURSELVES

When Yahusha returns, will He find *amanah* (steadfast obedience) on the Earth? Yes He will, and He is putting us to work in the harvest right now! We're Still Here Yahusha! We are doers of the Word, not hearers only. Those who think of themselves as Christians were originally known by a former label given to them by Yahusha when He said, "ANI HA GAFEN; ATAH HA NATSARIM."

Translated into English, it means, "I am the Vine; you are the NATSARIM," see Yn. 15:5

If you are doing the Word, or on the path to learning His Word, the adversary knows it. You will want to share this tract with Christian friends who do not yet know what Yahusha calls them.

Back To Our Hebrew Roots

Words mean important things. We were first known by a Hebrew word that started with the letter N; NATSARIM (Acts 24:5). 2000 years later, Yahusha's question at Luke 18 about finding AMANAH (belief, steadfast, obedience, trust) on the Earth helps us see how decadent and misguided our walk has become. AMANAH (steadiness, obedience) is the Hebrew word used at Kabaquq 2:4, and quoted at Galatians 3:11, Romans 1:17, and Hebrews 10:38. This relates directly to Yn. 8:31-32: "If you abide (live) in My Word, you are truly My talmidim, and you will know the Truth, and the Truth will set you free."

The prophet Kabaquq spoke of the time of the end, and told us so: Kabaquq 2:1-4: "I stand at my watch, and station myself on the watch-tower, and wait to see what He says to me, and what to answer when I am reproved. And Yahuah answered me and said, 'Write the vision and inscribe it on tablets, so that he who reads it runs. For the vision is yet for an appointed time, and it speaks of the end, and does not lie. If it lingers, wait for it, for it shall certainly come, it shall not delay. See, he whose being is not upright in him is puffed up. But the obedient one lives by his steadfastness (amanah).'"

If we live by every Word, as we see how far the world, as well as Christian pastors,

SIGNS ALL AROUND US

AUM
HINDU TRINITY

SHIVA & SHAKTI

GENOCIDE SYMBOL
LETTER N IN ARABIC

N IS FOR NATSARIM
SHATAN KNOWS WHO HE IS AFTER
CHRISTIANS ARE CALLED
NASRANI BY ARABS
NOTSRIM BY YAHUDIM
NATSARIM BY ACTS 24:5

GRAFTING IN
DO NOT CONSIDER YOURSELF SUPERIOR TO OTHERS

RESTORATION OF TWO STICKS

Yekezqal (Ez.) 37 speaks of the House of Yahudah and the House of Yisharal as two sticks (or trees). The book pictured at right was so thrilling for me to read, my heart leaped within me with joy after just a few pages into it. Yahual is about to do something that those who hear of it will feel their ears tingle; Kings will shut their mouths; they will see what they have not been told, and understand what they have not heard. (YashaYahu Is. 52) Yahuah scattered us, and promised to regather us from where He had scattered us among the foreigners. Yahuah scattered the tribes in order to bring deliverance to foreigners. Yasha'yahu (Is.) 49:6 and Acts 13:47 tells us why He mixed the tribes among all nations: to bring His deliverance to the ends of the Earth. Amos 9 verifies this. Now we see His plan is to awaken us to our heritage in the last days, and then re-gather us at the Second Exodus described at YirmeYahu 3. Yahuah has awakened hunters and fishers: "Therefore see, the Yamim (days) are coming, says Yahuah, when it is no longer said, 'Yahuah lives Who brought up the children of Yisharal from the land of Mitsrayim, but, Yahuah lives Who brought up the children of Yisharal from the land of the north and from all the lands where He had driven them. For I shall bring them back into their land I gave to their fathers. See, I am

Study of Two House Restoration of ISRAEL

N. B. Parrish

sending for many fishermen, says Yahuah, and they shall fish them. And after that I shall send for many hunters, and they shall hunt them from every mountain and every hill, and out of the holes of the rocks." YirmeYahu / Jer. 16:14-16

Our teachers are the source of all our confusion; they run to teach, but Yahuah did not send them. There are divisive issues of many kinds based on bigotry, genealogy, and men's philosophies causing great disturbance among those being called out of idolatry, and struggling to be restored to favor. The only thing a person can offer to Yahuah is their obedience to His Torah, since all else is chaff.

Some sample content of tracts you can download free (first pages shown here).
Or get them all quickly; there are over 100 tracts on the AMBASSADISC digital library.
Each tract is 4 pages, and formatted to print double-sided on a single sheet of paper.

THE DAY OF YAHUAH
THE EAGLES ARE COMING
DO YOU KNOW WHO THEY ARE?

Mat 24:28, 29: "For wherever the dead body is, there the eagles shall be gathered together. And immediately after the distress of those days the sun shall be darkened, and the moon shall not give its light, and the stars shall fall from the heaven, and the powers of the heavens shall be shaken."

"WHOEVER CALLS UPON THE NAME OF YAHUAH WILL BE DELIVERED" - Yoel (Joel) 2, Acts 2
The reason they will be delivered is:
THEY HAVE BEEN SEALED WITH THE NAME OF YAHUSHA, THE DELIVERER.
Our Owner places His Name on His property, so the REAPERS will not harm what belongs to Him

REAPER

THE MALAKIM
WILL APPEAR
ON THE DAY OF
THE COVERING:
YOM KAFAR
DAY OF JUDGMENT

Our Redeemer is on His way, and the fallen malakim know their time is short.
People believing in a pre-Trib rapture will make some adjustments in their expectations, and come to accept the reality unfolding around them.
Most of them today are Sun-day Sabbath people, and many are becoming Natsarim * - end-true harvest workers.
Our most important work during the time of distress will be to help them be restored to the Covenant of Yahuah - His Torah - the message of ABYahu.

page 1 of 4

KJV: A JABBERING LIP
AND A FOREIGN TONGUE

A "Black Swan Event" is a term used to describe an unforeseen event that comes as a surprise with major effects. It is impossible to predict, but with the benefit of hindsight it can be identified for what it is.
For over 400 years the KJV has trained the entire world to speak the English language.
Now a prophecy is being fulfilled: average people are learning the Hebrew Name of our Creator is Yahuah, not GOD or LORD. Furthermore, the evidence of a huge conspiracy to hide the Name is exposed.

A JABBERING LIP
LATIN VULGATE'S DOMINUS
KJV'S "THE LORD"

PUTTING THINGS IN ORDER

The first protestants remained Catholic; they only protested the head of the Kirche being the papacy. The KJV is an Anglican Catholic translation. The KJV was used to teach English to the whole world for 400 years. It was based on the Latin Vulgate, and now helps point out what was withheld from us.

SUNDAY ORIGINS
WORSHIP OF THE RISING SUN IN SUN TEMPLES

The first day of each week is called Sunday, and is a counterfeit sabbath invented by Constantine. His edict in 321 called it the "day of the Sun." Sunday worship is proxy-worship of satan, the adversary. This practice began with Nimrod, who after being slain was worshipped as the Sun.

INCENSE BURNER DEDICATED TO SHAMMASH

HEBREW PHONOLOGY
THE STUDY OF THE SOUND OF A LANGUAGE

STOP! Hey, what's that sound? Everybody look what's going down . . .
YahuaH tells us through the prophet ZefanYah they have done violence to His Torah. They also bent His language such that He promised to restore it:
Zep 3:9. "For then I shall turn to the peoples a clean lip so that they all call on the Name of Yahuah to serve Him with one shoulder." YashaYahu 52:5:
"Those who rule over them make them howl', declares Yahuah, 'and My Name is despised all day continually."
To Yahuah, we sound like we're howling.

HEBREW PHONOLOGY

THE GOAL IS TO RESTORE YAHUAH'S NAME TO OUR SPEECH

Some sample content of tracts you can download free (first pages shown here).
Or get them all quickly; there are over 100 tracts on the AMBASSADISC digital library.
Each tract is 4 pages, and formatted to print double-sided on a single sheet of paper.

ALEF-TAU

ANCIENT

ARAMAIC

TAU **ALEF**

The **first** and **last** letters of the Hebrew Alef-Beth are mysteriously placed near the Covenant Name (identity) of **Yahuah** throughout the Scriptures. It is an identity marker of the First and the Last, finally revealed by Yahusha ha'Mashiak as **Himself** at Rev. 1:8.

THE REVELATION OF YAHUSHA'S IDENTITY

The beast apparatus is the "world order" filled with deception for those who reject receiving a love for the Truth. For most of the past 2000 years, the influence of eastern mysticism and Gnostic "enlightenment" has dominated the western world. This *Gnosticism* has multiplied itself and is now seen *everywhere*, posing as the various forms of "religion," all posturing themselves to be the only "truth." At the core of them all is the worship of the "host of heaven" (Zodiac/ Astrology), originating in Babel's worship of *Nimrod, Semiramis, and Tammuz*. This is the premise of Alexander Hislop's book, *The Two Babylons*. The false worship of the sun, moon, and constellations (Zodiac, zoo animals) manifests itself in the *three heads*, and sometimes *triple pairs of arms* depicted in statues.

Beads, flowers, nimbuses (haloes), ashes (note forehead of image at right), and meditation positions are just a few of the aspects of Babel's false worship. The majority of the "church fathers" were originally followers of *Manichaeism*, a religion founded by **Mani** (216-277CE). Manichaeism was a major **Gnostic religion**, originating in Sassanid-era Babylonia.

Mani's Gnostic teachings about Yahusha became the pattern seen in many tenets of Christianity, adopted through the "church fathers." These pretenders are often referred to as "men of the cloth," wearing their special robes as we see with any other uniformed professional.

The people of Beroia (Acts 17) checked Scripture to validate everything they heard. Since that time, **Gnostic** beliefs were adopted, and it was taught that the Creator is THREE, not ONE as the *Shema* states. This has been promoted so well that *any who challenge that premise are regarded as heretics*. For a moment, let's think *outside that box* (prison, stronghold), and go with the working premise that the Creator is ONE, as He claims He is.

TRINITY CONFUSION

Since Yahusha declared that He and the Father are one, let's hypothetically take that statement at literally. If Yahuah entered into His physical world and *appeared* as one of us, that which we could see and touch of Him would be His "son" revealing Himself just as the opening words of Hebrews explain:

Heb 1:1-6: "**Alahim**, having of old spoken in many portions and many ways to the fathers by the prophets, has in these last days spoken to us (by or as) the **Son**, whom He has appointed heir of all, through whom also He made the ages, Who being the brightness of the esteem and the <u>exact</u> representation of His substance, and sustaining all by the Word of His power, having made a cleansing of our sins through Himself, sat down at the right hand of the Greatness on high, having become so much better than the messengers, as He has inherited a more excellent Name than them. For to which of the messengers did He ever say, 'You are My Son, today I have brought You forth?' And

Some sample content of tracts you can download free (first pages shown here). Or get them all quickly; there are over 100 tracts on the AMBASSADISC digital library. Each tract is 4 pages, and formatted to print double-sided on a single sheet of paper.

Is Your Mind Imprisoned?

Our enemy is not flesh and blood. When anyone awakens, their dreaming stops. The controller (beast) is losing, and has been on a downward spiral since Yahusha opened the eyes of His Natsarim. Undirected knowledge of the existence of the controller isn't enough; only the Truth can set us free.

Newly available printed or eBooks at Amazon
ALSO CHECK FOR THEM AT TORAHZONE.NET

While we are still here, you can order directly from here: **torahzone.net**
Because we're in our 70's, we've also put the books on Amazon for international orders because they are printed near the person ordering them. Also, when Yahusha takes us, they will still remain available. Amazon prints and distributes over 70 percent of the world's books at the moment, and makes them available as eBooks as well.

We would love to ship directly for you, but as I said we can only do what we can do - Yahusha has reminded us to number our days, and as Eccl. 9:10 advises, what your hand finds to do, do it with all your might - you can do nothing from sheol, where you are going.

Remember the three words this book started out to teach you? The First Commandment identifies WHO we are to obey, and to have no other.

He's looking for His *obedient* ones, so let's listen to *Him*, and no one else.

We now know we cannot trust the translators and teachers of tradition.

In the Preface of the NASB, they admit the Name is most significant, and it is inconceivable for anyone to think of not using the proper designation. Then, they explain they did what they said is inconceivable:

NASB - PRINCIPLES OF TRANSLATION

The Proper Name of God in the Old Testament: In the Scriptures, the name of God is most significant and understandably so. It is inconceivable to think of spiritual matters without a proper designation for the Supreme Deity. Thus the most common name for deity is God, a translation of the Hebrew *Elohim*. The normal word for Master is Lord, a rendering of *Adonai*. There is yet another name which is particularly assigned to God as His special or proper name, that is, the four letters YHWH (Exodus 3:14 and Isaiah 42:8). This name has not been pronounced by the Jews because of reverence for the great sacredness of the divine name. Therefore, it was consistently pronounced and translated Lord. The only exception to this translation of YHWH is when it occurs in immediate proximity to the word Lord, that is, *Adonai*. In that case it is regularly translated God in order to avoid confusion.

ᵞ𝐙ᗱᘿᒪ𝐀 ᗱᝐᗱ𝐙 𝐙ᵞ𝐘ᗱ
ANOKI YAHUAH ALAHIK
(I AM YAHUAH YOUR ALAH)

Yahusha will sing these words over us at His return. If you receive Him, you receive the One Who sent Him. He is Al Shaddai.

The Mark Of The Beast Is A Riddle

The solving of the riddle requires wisdom (see Prov. 1:6, Ps. 49:4).

Without wisdom, no one is able to solve the riddle at Rev. 13 that concerns "buying and selling."

Yahukanon's writings allude to a beast (behemoth), and the interpretation of the elements he describes are presented as a riddle to be solved.

He does not provide you with all the pieces to solve it, but points to how to find the missing components. Revelation 13:16-17 relates this riddle to be associated with "buying and selling."

Here is wisdom: let him who has understanding perform the calculation. Look at all the components, then add wisdom, and you solve it easily.

Wisdom is Torah, and gives the simple the ability to solve riddles.

The reason few know how to solve the riddle is they have no regard for Torah.

There is a veil over their minds regarding *Shabath. The sign forever between Yahuah and His people.*

fossilizedcustoms.com/mark.html

"My Aduni And My Alahim"

These words of Thomas are found at Yn. 20:28.

Philippians 2:10-11 has been veiled by the removal of the Name from translations.

Kurios / Dominus (Greek and Latin terms for LORD) were devices used to *replace* the Name of Yahuah (see they admit this in the Preface of your translation). It should read Every knee will bow and every tongue will admit that Yahuah is Yahusha ha Mashiak, to the esteem of the Father. He is one and the same essence as Abba.

Yahuah *is* Yahusha ha Mashiak, and at His first coming in the flesh, He reconciled mankind to Himself. At His second coming, He'll *stay forever.* He is Al Shaddai, the First and the Last (Rev. 1:8).

There's much, much more evidence in Scripture. Yahusha is omnipresent; can I get a witness? **fossilizedcustoms.com/omnipresence.html**

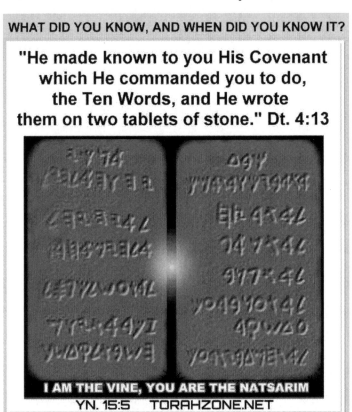

WHAT DID YOU KNOW, AND WHEN DID YOU KNOW IT?

"He made known to you His Covenant which He commanded you to do, the Ten Words, and He wrote them on two tablets of stone." Dt. 4:13

I AM THE VINE, YOU ARE THE NATSARIM

YN. 15:5   TORAHZONE.NET

DEDICATED TO ALL NATSARIM
The branches of the teachings of Yahusha have multiplied on Earth in recent years. They are vessels containing a precious treasure:
The living presence of the Creator of the universe.
The Spirit / Ruach of prophecy is the testimony of Yahusha, speaking through us. We don't know what we will say until the moment He chooses to give us the words others need to hear. Galatians 2:20 tells us,
"I no longer live, but Mashiak lives in me."

Hear Him.